NEW NELSON HISTORY

9|43 · 08|c

ERIC WILMOT

Acquisitions: Roda Morrison
Administration: Eileen Regan
Editorial: Catherine Dakin
Marketing: Jeremy Warner
Production: Ros Moon
Staff design: Lorraine Inglis
Typesetting: David La Grange

Thomas Nelson & Sons Ltd
Nelson House Mayfield Road
Walton-on-Thames Surrey
KT12 5PL UK

First published by
Thomas Nelson and Sons Ltd 1997

ɪⓉⱭ®   Thomas Nelson is an
       International Thomson Publishing Company

ɪⓉⱭ®   is used under licence

ISBN 0-17-435107-0
NPN 9 8 7 6 5 4 3 2

Acknowledgements
The publishers are grateful to the following for permission to reproduce
copyright material:
AKG Photo: pp. 6 (2), 8 (top left), 9 (centre), 11 (bottom), 16, 18 (top), 28, 29
(top), 32, 34, 38 (left and top right), 44 (right), 47 (centre), 48, 49, 50, 51, 56
(top 2), 57 (right), 58; Hulton Deutsch: pp. 11 (top), 12, 13 (bottom), 17, 18
(bottom), 19, 22 (top), 39 (top right), 56 (bottom), 57 (left), 60 (bottom);
Hulton Getty: pp. 7 (top right and bottom), 9 (top right); Image Select: pp. 7
(right), 8 (bottom right), 30 (top); Peter Newark: pp. 23 (centre), 30 (bottom);
The Photo Source: pp. 37; Popperfoto: pp. 8 (top right), 9 (top left), 13 (top), 23
(3), 29 (bottom), 38 (bottom right), 42, 45, 47, 60 (top), 62

Every effort has been made to trace all the relevant copyright holders, but if any
have been inadvertently overlooked, the publishers will be pleased to make the
necessary arrangements at the first opportunity.

Printed in Croatia

Contents

Overview

Germany 1918–1945

Germany began and ended this turbulent period of its history in defeat. This introduction surveys the key events in Germany between the ending of the two world wars.

page 13

ASSIGNMENT

The thirteen pictures on these pages have been arranged at random. The page number on each slide indicates where you can read more about the event in the following chapters. Your task is to create a slide show presentation using each of the thirteen pictures. Present the material in chronological order and give a short commentary on each picture.

page 7

page 9

page 7

page 23

page 21

page 36

page 47

page 27

page 34

page 44

page 13

page 38

The German Republic 1918–1929

Germany in defeat 1918

After its creation in 1871, the German Empire was ruled by a powerful monarch, the Kaiser. Germany had a parliament – the Reichstag – but elected politicians had very limited powers. Germany was governed chiefly by the Kaiser and his ministers.

In 1914, Germany went to war with Britain, France and Russia. By September 1918, the German generals were forced to admit that the war was lost. In order to shift responsibility for the lost war from the army to the politicians, however, they persuaded Kaiser Wilhelm II to transfer more power to the Reichstag. On 3 October 1918 a new, parliamentary government was formed with Prince Max von Baden as Chancellor. That same evening, the government appealed to the Allies for peace.

Kaiser Wilhelm II

The birth of the Weimar Republic

The admission of defeat came as a bombshell to the German public and sparked off weeks of troubles known as the **German Revolution**.

28 October 1918:
Mutiny of sailors at the Wilhelmshaven naval base. Mutiny spreads to other ports.

Sailors at Wihelmshaven, 1918.

3 November 1918:
The naval base at Kiel is taken over by sailors and soldiers.

6-8 November 1918:
Workers' and soldiers' councils take control of major cities including Hamburg, Berlin, Hanover, Cologne, Düsseldorf, Leipzig and Frankfurt.

Workers gather in Berlin, 1918.

7 November 1918:
Bavaria is seized by left-wing radicals and a socialist republic declared.

9 November 1918:
Strikes and demonstrations in Berlin. The Kaiser abdicates. Germany becomes a republic. A new government is formed under Friedrich Ebert.

Friedrich Ebert

11 November 1918:
Germany signs an armistice agreement (cease-fire).

The German delegation signing the armistice, 1918.

19 January 1919:
Elections are held for a new National Assembly.

6 February 1919:
The National Assembly meets at the town of Weimar. Ebert becomes President. The **Weimar Republic** is born.

Friedrich Ebert addressing the first meeting of the National Assembly at Weimar, 1919.

Street disturbances in Berlin, 1918.

Unstable Republic: the evidence

For the first five years, the German Republic had to fight for its life. It faced political enemies at home, a desperate financial situation, and open hostility from the French.

This section examines some of the major political challenges to the new German Republic.

1

The Spartacist Revolt 1919

The **Spartacists** were German Communists who aimed to build a Soviet Germany in alliance with Soviet Russia. Their leaders were Rosa Luxemburg (below) and Karl Liebknecht. From 5–11 January 1919, the Spartacists fought to seize control of Germany in an armed uprising. To combat this threat, the government encouraged the formation of **Freikorps** (anti-Communist volunteer units) and turned them loose on the Communists. The poorly organised Spartacists were crushed during bloody street battles in Berlin. On 15 January, Freikorps soldiers murdered Rosa Luxemburg and Karl Liebknecht.

2

Revolution in Bavaria 1918–19

In November 1918, left-wing extremists seized control of Bavaria and set up a socialist republic. Their leader was Kurt Eisner (right). Eisner was assassinated in February 1919 and Bavaria was taken over by the German Communist Party. Bavaria became a Soviet Republic and the Communists began to recruit a 'Red Army'. In May 1919, government troops and some Freikorps units, battled their way into Munich and brutally crushed the breakaway Republic.

A scene from the Spartacist Revolt, 1919.

3

The Kapp Putsch 1920

On 13 March 1920, right-wing extremists staged an armed rising (putsch) in Berlin. Freikorps units, led by General von Luttwitz, seized control of the capital and

named Wolfgang Kapp (left) as Germany's new leader. The German army refused to fire on the Freikorps, but the rising failed when Berlin workers staged a general strike in protest at the uprising and paralysed the city (see right). Millions of workers across Germany joined in the strike and on 18 March, Kapp and Luttwitz fled to Sweden.

4

The 'Red Army' of the Ruhr 1920

In some parts of Germany, workers on strike in protest at the Kapp Putsch began violent risings of their own. In the Ruhr region, a 'Red Army' was formed by socialist workers. The 'Red Army' controlled the Ruhr for several weeks before being defeated by government troops.

5

Right-wing murder squads 1921–22

After the Kapp Putsch, the Freikorps were disbanded. Right-wing radicals now set up illegal clubs and societies to carry on the fight against the Republic. They formed murder squads which carried out assassinations. Mathias Erzberger (leader of the Centre Party) and Walter Rathenau (the Foreign Minister) were both shot dead by right-wing terrorists belonging to a group known as the 'Consul Organisation'. Between 1919 and 1923, right-wing extremists carried out 354 political murders in Germany.

Mathias Erzberger

Walter Rathenau

Why was the German Republic so unstable in the years 1918–1923?

The shock of defeat

The German public was not prepared for defeat in World War I. Wartime propaganda had created the expectation of victory, so news of the surrender came as a terrible shock to the German people. Right-wing nationalists were outraged at the defeat and a popular myth developed that the 'undefeated' army had been 'stabbed in the back' by cowardly politicians who had arranged the cease-fire. Although a leading General, Ludendorff and the Army High Command had insisted that the government make peace, it was a politician, Mathias Erzberger who had headed the armistice delegation. The army washed its hands of all responsibility for the cease-fire and the new Republic became associated with defeat.

The anger of the nationalists reached boiling point in July 1919 when the terms of the Versailles peace treaty became known (see **Datapoint** below).

◄ D A T A P O I N T ►

Versailles: The Bitter Peace

Loss of territory

1 Alsace-Lorraine to France
2 Eupen and Malmedy to Belgium
3 Northern Schleswig to Denmark
4 Memel to Lithuania
5 Eastern Upper Silesia to Poland
6 Posen and West Prussia to Poland
7 The Rhineland to be occupied by Allied troops for 15 years
8 Danzig made a Free City under League of Nations control
9 The Saar placed under League of Nations control for 15 years
10 Germany forbidden to unite with fellow Germans in Austria
11 All overseas colonies taken from German control

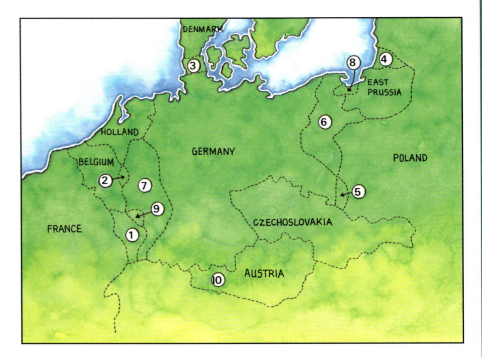

Military restrictions
- Army reduced to 100,000 men (smaller than the Belgian army)
- Navy reduced to 15,000 men
- Only six battleships allowed
- No submarines allowed
- No air force allowed
- No tanks allowed
- No heavy guns allowed
- Germany forbidden to build fortifications within 50 km east of the Rhine (close to the border with France)

Economic and financial losses
- 13% of German territory was lost
- six million Germans became citizens of other countries
- 20% of Germany's coal, iron and steel industry was lost
- 15% of Germany's agricultural production was lost
- The Saar coal mines were given to France
- Overseas investments were confiscated by the Allies
- Most of the German merchant fleet was taken by Britain
- Germany had to pay reparations (compensation payments) for damage caused during the war. The amount was fixed in 1921 at £6,600 million.

The impact of Versailles

The Treaty was greeted with shock and anger in Germany. Right-wing nationalists raged against the politicians who signed it and branded them the 'November Criminals'. The vast majority of Germans thought the Treaty harsh and humiliating. Apart from their objections to the terms of the Treaty (see **Datapoint Versailles: The Bitter Peace**) they felt bitter about the peace settlement for other reasons.

- Germans were not allowed a say in the making of the Treaty. They called it a dictated peace ('Diktat'). The German government had to accept the peace terms or face invasion.
- Germans felt that military restrictions undermined their security. Although Germany had to disarm, there were no guarantees that its enemies would do the same.

German delegates at Versailles, 1919.

- Article 231 of the Treaty has become known as the 'war guilt cause'. This part of the Treaty required Germany to take the blame for causing the war and for all the damage resulting from it. This was a bitter pill to swallow for Germans who believed they had been fighting a defensive war.
- Germans resented having to pay vast sums in reparations to countries which they believed shared the blame for causing the war.
- Germany signed the armistice on the understanding that the peace would be based on President Wilson's 'Fourteen Points'. This did not happen. The right of self-determination was denied to millions of Germans who now found themselves being governed by Poles, Czechs and Danes. Germans in East Prussia were completely cut off from the rest of Germany by a strip of land known as the 'Polish Corridor'.
- Germans had expected to be made full members of the new League of Nations. Germany was refused membership. This showed that Germany was not trusted and would not be given equal status with the victorious powers. The German public regarded this as a national insult.

Further problems

The shock of defeat and the humiliation of Versailles were not the only problems facing the new Republic. Consider these other factors:

- Left-wing extremists were hostile to the Republic because they felt it was too moderate. The Left wanted to turn Germany into a socialist state.
- The army was unreliable. Many officers were still loyal to the Kaiser and shared the view that Germany had been 'stabbed in the back'. The army was also biased towards the Right. During the Kapp Putsch, the army refused to take action against the nationalists. In the same year however, they did not hesitate to smash the 'Red Army' of the Ruhr.
- German judges often showed right-wing sympathies. Harsh punishments for political crimes were reserved for left-wing extremists. Right-wing offenders, however, were given very lenient treatment.
- There were six major political parties in Weimar Germany. No party ever won a majority so the Republic was ruled by coalition governments. After 1920, no coalition had a majority. There were disagreements within these coalitions and they faced fierce opposition from groups like the Communists and Nationalists who refused to work with them.

Invasion and Hyperinflation

The Republic inherited serious financial problems in 1918. The Kaiser's government had financed the war with massive borrowing and by printing more money. This caused high inflation. After the war, the Republic continued these policies and, eventually, the value of the currency tumbled. The financial crisis deepened in 1921 when Germany was presented with a huge reparations bill of £6,600 million. The government handed over the first instalment but in 1922, announced that it could pay no more. The French reaction was swift. In January 1923, French and Belgian troops crossed the Rhine and occupied the Ruhr, Germany's premier industrial region. The French intended to help themselves to the vast resources of the area.

Germany was suddenly united in anger at the actions of the French. The German government called on the people of the Ruhr to offer 'passive, resistance' to the invaders. As a result, the Ruhr was paralysed by a general strike and there were violent clashes between French troops and the Ruhr strikers.

Passive resistance crippled the already fragile German economy. Even before the French invasion, high inflation had made the mark almost worthless (see **Datapoint: Hyperinflation**). In 1923 the situation escalated out of control. The government had to pay

French troops take control of the General Post Office, Düsseldorf, 1923.

the striking workers and, because there were no coal deliveries from the Ruhr, it had to buy foreign coal with valuable reserves of foreign currency. In addition, tax revenue from the Ruhr dried up. By April 1923, the government was spending seven times more than it received in revenue. Its answer was to print more money which created a nightmare situation known as **hyperinflation** (see **Datapoint: Hyperinflation**).

The solution

In August 1923, a new government was formed. Gustav Stresemann became Chancellor. In September, Stresemann called off passive resistance and resumed reparations payments. A new currency, the Rentenmark, was introduced in November and the old currency was scrapped. As inflation was bought under control, the government faced new political threats. In October, a planned Communist revolution in Saxony was crushed by the army. In Bavaria, right-wing nationalists, enraged by the ending of passive resistance, staged an armed rising in Munich (see page 23). The rising was a failure, but for the first time, it brought national attention to one of its leaders; a young and ambitious ex-soldier by the name of Adolf Hitler.

Gustav Stresemann

A shopkeeper uses a tea chest to hold money during the hyperinflation of 1923.

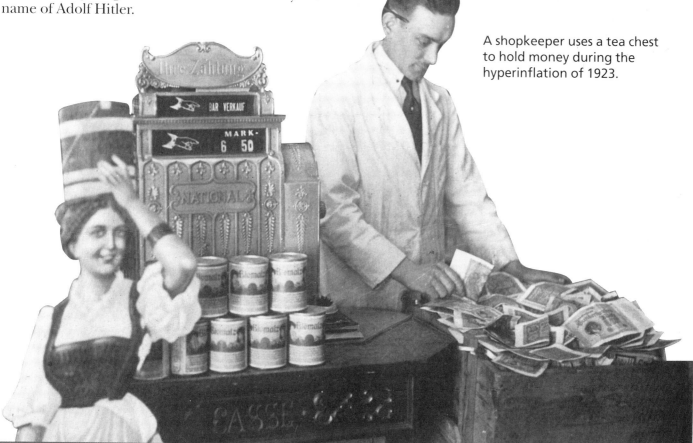

Hyperinflation

Definition: A situation in which the value of money falls extremely quickly until it becomes worthless. In hyperinflation situations, it is common for people to resort to the bartering (exchanging) of goods and services.

Value of the German mark (marks to the dollar)

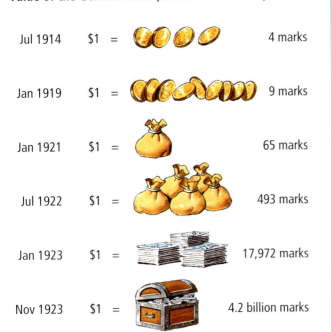

Jul 1914	$1 =		4 marks
Jan 1919	$1 =		9 marks
Jan 1921	$1 =		65 marks
Jul 1922	$1 =		493 marks
Jan 1923	$1 =		17,972 marks
Nov 1923	$1 =		4.2 billion marks

 0·54

 165·5

The price of a loaf of bread

Dec 1918	0.54
Dec 1921	3.9
Dec 1922	165.5
Mar 1923	463
Sep 1923	1,512,000
Nov 1923	201,000,000,000

Source Investigation

Why did Germany surrender?

'We can carry on the war for a substantial further period, we can cause the enemy heavy loss…but we cannot win the war. We must make up our minds to abandon the war as hopeless. Every day brings the enemy nearer to his goal….'

General Ludendorff, leading General and chief adviser to Field Marshal Hindenburg 1916–18, speaking on 29 September, 1918.

SOURCE B

'...we could have brought the struggle to a favourable conclusion if...co-operation had existed between the army and those at home. But while the enemy showed an even greater will for victory, divergent party interests began to show themselves with us.... As an English General has said, "The Germany army was stabbed in the back". No blame is to be attached to the sound core of the army.... It is plain enough on whom the blame lies.'

General Hindenburg speaking in November, 1919. Hindenburg was Field Marshal of the German army, 1916–18.

General von Hindenburg (centre) with German officers.

SOURCE C

'By November 1918 the German army was close to total collapse though it still occupied French and Belgian soil. Socialist propaganda was spreading among the troops and morale was beginning to break down. On 28 September, Ludendorff informed the government that complete victory was still possible, but that the breakdown of the home front and the spread of defeatism were letting down the army. On the 29th he informed them that the war was lost and advised an immediate...appeal to the Allies for a peace settlement.'

Michael Hughes, *Nationalism and Society: Germany 1800–1945* (1988). Michael Hughes is a lecturer in history.

QUESTIONS

1 Study source B. This is an explanation of the German surrender in 1918. How useful do you think it is? Explain your answer.

2 Study sources A and B. These sources describe Germany's situation in 1918 in different ways. How would you account for the differences in these accounts?

3 Study sources B and C. Which of these sources gives the more reliable explanation for the German surrender in 1918?

1924–29 Weimar's 'golden' years?

Read any textbook account of Weimar in the Twenties and you could be forgiven for thinking that the Republic had overcome its early problems and become firmly established in Germany. The talk in such accounts is of 'stability', 'prosperity' and 'international respectability'. Yet this image is misleading. Beneath the calm and prosperous surface lurked problems and weaknesses which threatened to destroy the fragile Republic. This section explores the two faces of Weimar's 'golden' years.

Prosperity

After the nightmare of hyperinflation, German industry and agriculture flourished. The new currency brought stability and removed the fear of inflation. The Dawes Plan (see page 18) made reparations more manageable and there was massive foreign investment. Between 1924 and 1930, 25.5 billion marks were pumped into the German economy, most of it from American banks. As new factories were built and older ones modernised, industrial production expanded. New houses, shops and cinemas were built. Unemployment fell and living standards improved. Germany's share of world trade increased and by 1929, exports were 34 per cent greater than they had been in 1913.

Political stability

During the 'golden' Twenties, mainstream politics was dominated by the democratic parties. The extreme right, which included Hitler's Nazis, were kept firmly on the outside looking in. The Communists did slightly better, but at this stage, they were still unable to make a serious impact upon the Republic. The coalition government appeared to be performing well and to have the confidence of the German people .

Election results 1924–28	May 1924	Dec 1924	May 1928
Social Democrats	100	131	153
Nationalists	95	103	73
Communists	62	45	54
Nazis	32	14	12

Note: this source does not show the results of all political parties in these years

'Dancing on a volcano'

'The economic position is only flourishing on the surface. Germany is in fact dancing on a volcano. If the short term credits [loans] are called in [by America], a large section of our economy would collapse.'

Gustav Stresemann, speaking shortly before his death in 1929.

German prosperity was built on quicksand foundations. The Weimar economy depended upon high-interest American loans which usually had to be repaid or renewed within three months. This was fine in good times, but if American lenders came under pressure they could demand rapid repayment and stop renewing the vital loans. It was a very dangerous situation indeed.

Many Germans did not share in the prosperity of the 'golden' years. Unemployment never fell below 1.3 million in spite of the economic recovery. Although big business grew in the Twenties, small

General Paul von Hindenburg (right) with Kaiser Wilhelm II in 1915.

1920s Berlin.

firms and retailers struggled. Unable to compete, many faced the threat of bankruptcy. Higher wages and new national insurance contributions placed further strains on small businesses. By the end of 1927 some sections of the German economy were already in trouble. A world-wide agricultural depression caused agricultural prices to fall and many farmers began to sink into debt. In the winter of 1928–29 unemployment soared to nearly three million.

Political opposition

The majority of Germans had little genuine enthusiasm for the Republic. Most co-operated with it only because there was no real alternative. Many openly despised the Republic and there were repeated calls in the Twenties for 'stronger' government. The nationalists were the main critics of the Republic but other groups, including the army, the civil service, industrialists, judges and the universities, favoured the old Imperial government. It was no coincidence that in 1925, Field Marshal Hindenburg, hero of the Kaiser's army and devout believer in the 'stab in the back' theory, was elected President of the Republic. In Berlin, he was greeted by cheering crowds waving black, white and red flags, the colours of the old Empire. Hindenburg never identified himself with the Republic and remained loyal to the exiled Kaiser. His election did nothing to rally support behind the Republic.

Other political groups, notably the Communists, wanted to destroy the Republic and replace it with a socialist government. Support for the Communists increased steadily during the Twenties, especially from the German working classes. Only when times were good could the Republican parties hope to control Germany. Their coalitions were unstable and no party had a majority during the entire Weimar period. There was always the possibility that a crisis could de-stabilise the Republic and open the floodgates of opposition.

Reparations

The reparations figure set in 1921 was clearly excessive. Germany could not pay and the consequences of the Ruhr invasion forced the international community to re-consider the sum. In 1924 a new reparations scheme, the Dawes Plan, was introduced by Charles Dawes. The total figure remained the same as that set in 1921, but payments were to be made strictly on the basis of what Germany could afford. No date was set for the final settlement of the reparations bill. For the first four years Germany would make reduced payments. Large overseas loans were made available to help Germany pay and to stimulate the economy.

The Dawes Plan was a significant development in the reparations saga. The Allies now appeared to understand that Germany could only pay if its economy was allowed to recover and that this would

Charles Dawes

'A second Versailles'

The Dawes and Young Plans were savaged by right-wing nationalists. To them, the payment of reparations was an admission that Germany had caused the war, an accusation which they passionately disputed. They resented the Dawes Plan because it gave the Allies partial control over Germany's railways and the German State Bank. The nationalists called the Dawes Plan 'a second Versailles'. The Young Plan met with similar opposition. Nationalists were appalled that the government had agreed to continue paying out for a further 59 years. They accused the government of selling Germany's children into slavery to the Allies. Alfred Hugenburg, the new leader of the German Nationalist Party, organised a referendum against the Young Plan, supported by Hitler's Nazis. He called for any politician signing it to be thrown in jail. Nearly six million Germans voted against the Young Plan, though this fell far short of the 21 million votes needed.

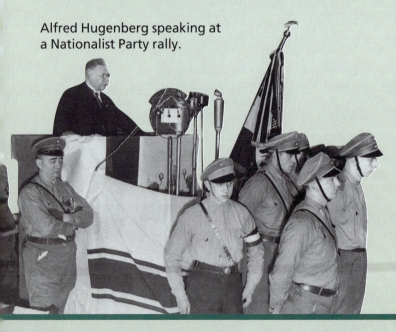

Alfred Hugenberg speaking at a Nationalist Party rally.

QUESTIONS

1 What were the main achievements of Stresemann's foreign policy in the period 1924–29?

2 To what extent were the arrangements regarding reparations changed between 1921 and 1929?

3 Had Germany accepted the Treaty of Versailles by the 1920s?

4 What did Stresemann mean when he said that Germany was 'dancing on a volcano'?

5 Do the election results on p.16 prove that there was political stability in Germany from 1924–29?

6 '1924–29 were "golden years" for the Weimar Republic'. Do you accept this conclusion? Explain your answer carefully.

only happen if it were not burdened with excessive reparations. Further progress was made in 1929 with the adoption of the Young Plan. This went further by cutting the amount Germany had to pay to less than one third of the figure set in 1921. Annual payments of about 2000 million Reichsmarks would be made until 1988. In return for accepting the plan, the Allies agreed to evacuate the Rhineland in 1930, five years ahead of schedule.

International co-operation

Gustav Stresemann was perhaps the most able statesman of the Weimar years. Although he was Chancellor for a short time in 1923 (August-November), it was as Foreign Minister from 1924 to 1929 that he is best remembered. Under Stresemann, Germany broke out of the diplomatic isolation of the early post-war years and came to be accepted as a

valuable and trusted member of the international community. In 1925 Germany joined with France and Belgium to sign the Locarno Pact. They agreed to respect their mutual frontiers and to accept the League of Nations rulings on any disputes. Germany agreed that the Rhineland should remain demilitarised and France promised not to send troops onto German soil again as she had done during the Ruhr crisis. In 1926 Germany was welcomed into the League of Nations and in 1928 along with 64 other nations, signed the Kellog-Briand Pact, thereby promising to settle disputes without resorting to war. Germany appeared to have accepted the Treaty of Versailles and seemed committed to the new ideals of peace and international co-operation.

Stresemann making a speech to the League of Nations in Geneva, 1926.

Stresemann's deeper motives

Signatures on treaties and friendly handshakes could not mask the deep suspicions which continued to plague relations between Germany and its neighbours. Although Stresemann spoke of a 'new era of co-operation among the nations', it was clear that he had not accepted the Treaty of Versailles and was determined to dismantle it. Stresemann was a nationalist and his main aim in foreign policy was to restore Germany's status as a great power. He was committed to a thorough revision of the Treaty of Versailles. In these aims he was no different to extremists like Hitler but, unlike Hitler, Stresemann

understood the need to work with the Allies rather than to fight them. The reality was that in the Twenties, Germany was weak. There was little point in being aggressive, but through negotiation and co-operation Stresemann hoped to make cautious progress towards a revision of the Treaty. Thus when he signed the Locarno Pact, he did so partly because he hoped it would lead to an early evacuation of the Rhineland. When he attended meetings of the League of Nations after 1926, he used these occasions to air German grievances on the international stage. At the same time, Germany was secretly and illegally rearming. The Treaty of Rapallo which Germany signed with Soviet Russia in 1922 led to secret military co-operation. Germany built factories in Russia which produced airplanes, tanks and poison gas. It trained military personnel and tested weapons on Russian soil. Although not on a large scale, this rearmament was strictly forbidden by the Treaty of Versailles. More significant was the fact that Stresemann made no guarantees at Locarno to respect the eastern frontiers with Poland and Czechoslovakia. Stresemann hoped that by gradually improving relations with the West, he would be allowed to make changes to Germany's eastern frontiers.

In spite of the public co-operation, the French remained nervous of Germany and they took no chances. During the Twenties, they continued with their plans to build massive fortifications, such as the Maginot Line on the Rhine frontier. They maintained alliances with Germany's eastern neighbours and supplied them with military aid. Old fears could not easily be forgotten.

3 Hitler and the Rise of the Nazis

Nazi Election Results 1924–1932

May 1924

Total number of Reichstag seats:	472
Number of Nazi voters:	1,918,000
Number of Nazi seats:	32
Nazi share of poll:	6.5%

Dec 1924

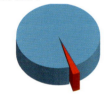

Total number of Reichstag seats:	493
Number of Nazi voters:	907,000
Number of Nazi seats:	14
Nazi share of poll:	3%

May 1928

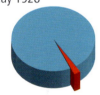

Total number of Reichstag seats:	491
Number of Nazi voters:	810,000
Number of Nazi seats:	12
Nazi share of poll:	2.6%

Sept 1930

Total number of Reichstag seats:	577
Number of Nazi voters:	6,409,000
Number of Nazi seats:	107
Nazi share of poll:	18.3%

July 1932

Total number of Reichstag seats:	608
Number of Nazi voters:	13,745,000
Number of Nazi seats:	230
Nazi share of poll:	37.3%

Nov 1932

Total number of Reichstag seats:	584
Number of Nazi voters:	11,737,000
Number of Nazi seats:	196
Nazi share of poll:	33.1%

Between May 1924 and November 1932 there were six general elections in Germany. The Datapoint on the left shows how the Nazi Party performed in each of these elections.

1 Describe the performance of the Nazi Party at the Reichstag elections during the Stresemann years (1924–29)

2 What was significant about the performance of the Nazis in the Reichstag elections of September 1930?

3 Why would it be important to find out what happened in Germany between May 1928 and September 1930?

4 What do you notice about the performance of the Nazis in the Reichstag elections of 1932?

5 A political party gains a majority in parliament when it wins more seats than all the other parties put together. Did the Nazis ever win a majority in the Reichstag?

Franz von Papen (centre) as Vice Chancellor.

Turning point – Chancellor Hitler

On 30 January 1933 Adolf Hitler, the leader of the Nazi Party, became Chancellor of Germany. Hitler did not take power by force in 1933, and he wasn't elected. His party never won a majority in the Reichstag and by the end of 1932, the Nazi vote was actually falling. Hitler was *appointed* to the chancellorship by President Hindenburg in an effort to break a frustrating political stalemate caused by the collapse of the Weimar Republic.

The Great Depression produced a crisis in Germany which the Weimar politicians proved unable to solve. The coalition government broke down and when the Nazis and Communists refused to participate in any further coalitions, parliamentary government ceased to function. From 1930, therefore, the ageing President Hindenburg used his powers to take charge of Germany and to rule by emergency decree. Hindenburg was manipulated by an ambitious army leader, Kurt von Schleicher into appointing a series of tame Chancellors who would carry out the wishes of the army. The first of these was Heinrich Bruning who became Chancellor in March 1930. Bruning fronted the government for two years ruling with emergency decrees signed by Hindenburg. Bruning was replaced in May 1932 by Franz von Papen.

In the Reichstag elections of July 1932, the Nazis won 230 seats making them the largest party in parliament. Hitler demanded that he should be given the position of Chancellor. Hindenburg, who did not trust Hitler and thought him unsuitable for the post of Chancellor, refused his request. The government continued to be led by von Papen but had little popular support. Fresh elections in November 1932 worried Hitler. The Nazis remained the largest party in the Reichstag with 196 seats but two million voters had deserted them.

Heinrich Bruning (right)

Hitler's bid for the chancellorship was again refused by Hindenburg.

In December, von Papen was dismissed and Kurt von Schleicher, the man who had been manipulating the President since 1930, became Chancellor himself. This was the development which gave Hitler his chance. Von Papen was determined to take revenge on von Schleicher. He began secret negotiations with Hitler offering him a share of power in a Hitler-von Papen government. Hitler agreed, but Hindenburg continued to oppose Hitler's appointment as Chancellor. Von Papen, who was a close friend of the President, persuaded him to reconsider. He argued that Hitler could be easily controlled by restricting the number of Nazi ministers and ensuring that the majority of cabinet

Kurt von Schleicher

members were Hitler's political rivals. In this way, the proposal was made to look very attractive. Germany would get a government with a majority in parliament and a Chancellor whose freedom of movement would be restricted by allies of von Papen and Hindenburg. The deal was done. Von Schleicher was dismissed and on 30 January, 1933 Hitler became Chancellor.

Hindenburg appointing Hitler as Chancellor, 1933.

Hitler and the Nazis: the early years

The Nazi Party began life as the German Workers' Party on 9 January, 1919. It was led by Anton Drexler and Karl Harrer and its meeting place was a pub in the Bavarian city of Munich. On 12 September 1919, a 30-year-old ex-soldier by the name of Adolf Hitler gave a short but powerful speech at the Party's monthly meeting. Drexler recruited him on the spot. By the end of the year Hitler had become head of propaganda. Two years later he was leading the Party.

Hitler was the son of an Austrian customs official. Before World War I he had been a drifter leading a miserable existence in the doss houses of Vienna and it was during this time that his political ideas developed. Hitler was proud of his German identity and was intensely nationalistic. He attacked Communists and Jews as evil forces working to undermine the German nation.

World War I provided the first real purpose to his life and when it ended in 1918, he was devastated. Hitler never accepted Germany's defeat and he resented the Weimar politicians who had signed the Treaty of Versailles. Once in the German Workers' Party, Hitler quickly revealed his special talent for public speaking (see source 2).

Under Hitler's influence, membership of the Party began to grow. In 1921 armed paramilitary squads were formed to protect Party meetings from disruption by opponents. These were the 'Stormtroopers', the SA. With brown uniforms and military discipline, the SA appealed to ex-soldiers and members of the outlawed Freikorps. The Stormtroopers protected Nazi meetings, assisted in propaganda activities and disrupted the meetings of rival parties.

Anton Drexler

1

'[The SA] is intended to bind our young party members together to form an organisation of iron, so that it may put its strength at the disposal of the whole movement to act as a battering ram.'

Part of a statement in the Nazi newspaper the *Volkischer Beobachter* 3 August, 1921.

'As a member of the stormtroop of the NSDAP I pledge myself by its storm flag: to be always ready to stake life and limb in the struggle for the aims of the movement; to give absolute military obedience to my military superiors and leaders.'

Part of the oath of loyalty which every new Stormtrooper recruit was required to make.

2

'I do not know how to describe the emotions that swept over me as I heard this man....When he spoke of the disgrace of Germany, I felt ready to spring on any enemy....I forgot everything but the man; then glancing around, I saw that his magnetism was holding these thousands as one....I experienced an exhaltation that could be likened only to religious conversion.'

Kurt Ludecke after seeing Hitler speak in 1922.

The Munich Putsch

By 1923 Munich had become a hotbed of right-wing agitation. The French invasion of the Ruhr and soaring inflation focused the anger of German nationalists on the 'feeble' Republic which seemed to be leading Germany from one catastrophe to another. Hitler pounced on this opportunity to kick the Republic while it was down. In November he attempted to seize power in Munich, the first stage of an ambitious plan to replace Weimar with a right-wing dictatorship. The putsch was a dismal failure. The army and the police could not be persuaded to support the Nazis, Hitler was arrested and his party was banned. In February 1924 he was put on trial for treason. His performance in the dock however, turned the trial into a propaganda triumph. Hitler's defiant justification of the putsch made him a hero with German nationalists. The judges sympathised with Hitler's motives and he was given the minimum sentence available – five years detention in Landsberg prison. By Christmas, he had been freed and, two months later he re-founded the Nazi Party.

Following his release from prison, Hitler took his first steps on the legal path to power. At first, few Germans could be persuaded to vote for the Nazis. By 1930 however, they were backing him in their millions. What happened to produce this spectacular reversal of fortune can be examined in the rest of this chapter.

3

Hitler used his time in prison to write a book which he called *Mein Kampf* (My Struggle). The book became the gospel of the Nazi Party. By 1940 sales had reached six million.

4

During his time in prison, Hitler gave up his plan to seize power by force and announced a new strategy:

'Instead of working to achieve power by armed conspiracy, we shall have to hold our noses and enter the Reichstag.... If outvoting them takes longer than outshooting them, at least the results will be guaranteed by their own constitution!... Sooner or later we shall have a majority and after that we shall have Germany.'

Why did the Nazis attract little support in the years 1924–28?

Hitler re-founded the Nazi Party in February 1925 and began the task of winning power through the ballot box. Thirty-one million Germans voted in the elections of May 1928, just 810,000 of them supported the Nazis. William Shirer, an American journalist living in Germany at this time, passed this verdict on the Nazis:

> 'Nazism appeared to be a dying cause. It had mushroomed on the country's misfortunes [hyperinflation and the Ruhr invasion]; now that the nation's outlook was suddenly bright it was rapidly withering away....One scarcely heard of Hitler or the Nazis except as butts of jokes.'

From 1925 to 1928 the Nazis were in the political wilderness, a fringe party without influence, and apparently without hope. The main reason for this was the success of Stresemann's policies. After the crisis years of 1918–1924, Germany now seemed to be prosperous and stable. Unemployment was low and its international status was much improved. In these circumstances, extremist Nazi ideas had little appeal. Most Germans were happy to support the established democratic parties.

The Nazi Party also had an image and identity problem in this period. The Nazis believed that success would come if they could win mass support from industrial workers. Accordingly, Party organisers began to stress the 'socialist' ideas of Nazism in propaganda targeted at Germany's major industrial centres. But this strategy failed on two counts. Firstly, the bulk of the industrial working class remained loyal to the Communists and the Social Democrats which meant that Nazi propaganda fell largely on deaf ears. Secondly, by emphasising their socialist identity, the Nazis created the image of being a radical working class party. This isolated them from the middle classes who regarded the Nazis with suspicion and therefore continued to support the traditional parties.

If the Nazis were to achieve a political breakthrough they needed two things:

1 a new campaign strategy
2 a national crisis which they could exploit as they had done in 1923.

During 1928–1930, the Nazis got what they needed and their vote rocketed.

Nazi Voters

Region	Description
1 East Prussia	Rural economy - mainly Protestant - small towns
2 Berlin	Large city - industrial and commercial economy
3 Bavaria (Upper and Lower)	Overwhelmingly Catholic
4 Düsseldorf (East and West)	Industrial economy - large urban centres - mainly Catholic
5 Cologne-Aachen	Industrial economy - large urban centres
6 Pomerania	Rural economy - mainly Protestant- small towns
7 Schleswig Holstein	Rural economy - mainly Protestant - small towns
8 Koblenz	Rural economy - mainly Catholic
9 Westphalia	Industrial economy - large urban centres
10 Mecklenberg	Rural economy - mainly Protestant - small towns

QUESTIONS

1 **Complete the two sentences below using a selection of words from the boxed menu.**

(a) The Nazis performed best in regions which contained...

(b) The Nazis did worst in regions which contained...

> heavy industry - Protestants - big cities - Catholics - small towns - farming communities

◀ **D A T A P O I N T** ▶

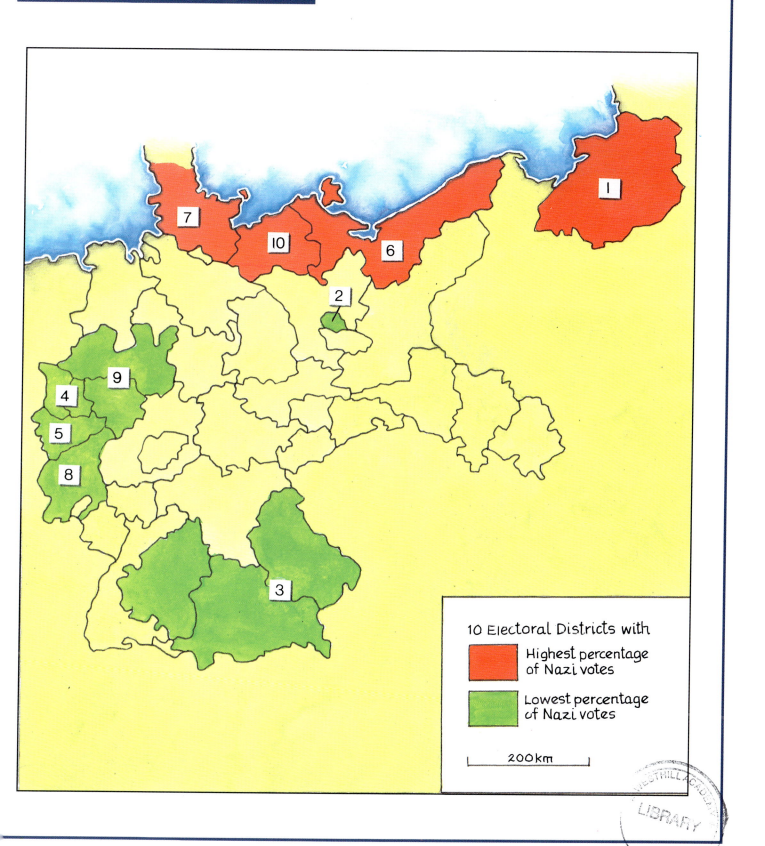

10 Electoral Districts with

Highest percentage of Nazi votes

Lowest percentage of Nazi votes

200km

Why did German voters support the Nazis after 1928?

In September 1930, a staggering 6.4 million Germans voted for the Nazis. With 107 seats the Nazis were now the second largest party in parliament. This astonishing transformation was the result of good fortune and careful planning.

New directions

During the local elections of 1927–28, the Nazis did very well in the agricultural regions of Schleswig-Holstein and Lower Saxony. Farmers here had been badly hit by an agricultural depression which had caused prices to fall and debts to rise. The Nazis exploited the misery of the farmers. Success in these elections led the Nazis to develop a new political strategy from 1928. Attention was turned away from the industrial working classes and was focused instead on rural workers and the middle class. The new strategy worked wonders, as the following Nazi newspaper explains.

The election results from the rural areas in particular have proved that with a smaller expenditure of energy, money and time, better results can be achieved there than in the big cities. In small towns and villages mass meetings with good speakers are events and are often talked about for weeks, while in the big cities the effects of meetings with even three or four thousand people soon disappear.

From an article in the *Volkischer Beobachter*, 31 May 1928.

As well as targeting a new audience, the Nazis also took steps to improve the Party's image and to give it a higher profile. In 1929, Hitler took his party into partnership with the German Nationalist Party, led by Alfred Hugenberg to oppose the Young Plan (see page 18). This move rapidly changed the image of the Nazis. They now became associated with a respectable and conservative party with a long tradition in German politics. The Nazis ceased to be seen as a radical, working class party and thus became more attractive to middle class voters. The association with Hugenberg brought other advantages too. Hugenberg was a powerful figure in the German newspaper industry. In 1927 he expanded his media empire by buying Ufa, Germany's largest film company. Suddenly, the Nazis found themselves thrust into the political limelight. Hugenberg's newspapers reported Nazi activities and Ufa newsreels recorded Nazi rallies. When they were screened to audiences in the extensive network of Ufa cinemas, the Nazis found attention and publicity on a national scale.

A war veteran begging in the street in Hanover during the Depression, 1930.

Depression and crisis

In October 1929, the collapse of the American Stock Exchange exposed the vulnerable and fragile Weimar economy. The world sank into economic depression and Germany, now without the support of American loans, sank further than most. Unemployment soared from 1.5 million in October 1929 to 4.3 million in December 1930. The prices of agricultural products and consumer goods slumped causing financial hardship for farmers, small businesses and the self-employed. Food shortages, homelessness, high taxation, strikes and demonstrations added to the misery of millions of Germans.

The Weimar politicians appeared to have no solutions, but Hitler had plenty. The Nazis promised to protect farmers against foreign competition and to reduce taxes. They promised to create work for the unemployed, protect big business from Communism and to restore the middle class to their former status as the 'backbone of the nation'. In the circumstances of 1930, Nazi promises gave hope to millions of Germans who felt betrayed and deserted by the Republic. Large sections of the middle class and the rural workforce now turned their backs on the liberal parties and moved towards the Right. Support for the Nazis multiplied at an astonishing rate.

A dole queue in Hanover, 1930.

German soldiers serve soup from their field kitchen to the unemployed and destitute, 1931.

The power of propaganda

'All effective propaganda must be limited to a very few points and must harp on these in slogans until the last member of the public understands what you want him to understand.'

Hitler, *Mein Kampf* (1924).

Nazi propaganda was powerful and effective. The Nazi message was contained in simple slogans like *'ein Volk, ein Reich, ein Führer'* (One People, One Nation, One Leader). Nazi propaganda penetrated the minds of millions of Germans and helped the Party to win votes. The success of Nazi propaganda was due largely to the way the Party organised itself. Between 1925 and 1929 dedicated activists had established the Party at a local level throughout Germany. Most other parties were slower to see the potential of local organisation. When the Depression struck in 1929, the Nazis were ready to exploit the problems of Germans in all parts of the country. The methods they used can be explored in the sources on these pages.

1

The Nazis had a selection of newspapers under their control. To reach a wide audience, each paper had its own character and was designed to appeal to its own readership. The *Volkischer Beobachter* (National Observer) was a popular national daily which carried news items on popular Nazi themes such as the dangers of Communism. By contrast, *Der Sturmer* appealed to the hooligan element. It was viciously anti-Semitic and used crude language.

Translation: Women! Save the German family, vote for Adolf Hitler!

Translation: Work, Freedom and Bread!

2

The Nazis used massive poster campaigns to drive home their political message. The posters targeted different audiences and were timed to have maximum impact. In the following memo, written during the presidential elections of 1932, Goebbels explains to local propaganda departments when to put up a particular poster of Hitler:

'The Hitler poster depicts a fascinating Hitler head on a completely black background....In accordance with the Führer's wish, this poster is to be put up only during the final days [of the campaign]. Since experience shows that during the final days there is a variety of coloured posters, this poster with its completely black background will contrast with all the others and will produce a tremendous effect on the masses.'

3

Josef Goebbels (left) was appointed head of propaganda in 1929. Under his direction, Nazi propaganda became increasingly sophisticated. Film shows brought Nazi ideas to mass cinema audiences and the radio began to be used to broadcast the Nazi message. He organised massive press and poster campaigns and the distribution of free newspapers.

Middle-class citizens! Retailers! Craftsmen! Tradesmen!

A new blow aimed at your ruin is being prepared and carried out in Hanover!

The present system enables the giant concern WOOLWORTH (America)...to build a new vampire business in the centre of the city...Put an end to this system...Defend yourself, middle-class citizen! Join the mighty organisation that alone is in a position to conquer your arch-enemies. Fight with us in the Section for Craftsmen and Retail Traders within the great freedom movement of Adolf Hitler.

Nazi Party leaflet, April 1932.

4

The main feature of Nazi propaganda was the public meeting. Speakers were given cars to enable them to cover a large area at speed. They were paid according to the number of speeches they made – a powerful incentive to address as many meetings as possible. Propaganda squads targeted particular locations and spent days winning over the people with plays, concerts, sporting events and even church parades. Subjects for public meetings were carefully chosen to suit the audience. Local issues were investigated in advance and ruthlessly exploited as in the case of a plan to build a new department store in Hanover in this Nazi Party leaflet.

A Nazi public meeting.

The key issues

Nazi propaganda was powerful and effective because it concentrated on issues which millions of Germans felt close to. In their election campaigns, the Nazis attacked the Treaty of Versailles and promised to restore Germany's status as a leading world power. They led a furious assault against Communism and promised to repair the damaged economy.

The Nazis claimed to stand for national unity, strong leadership, discipline and order. They stood up for traditional moral and family values and savagely criticised the Weimar Republic for its betrayal and neglect of Germany. These ideas were highly attractive to Germans who desperately wanted a way out of the terrible crisis of the early 1930s. The Nazis had the advantage of not being associated with any of the Weimar governments. Since many Germans blamed the Weimar parties for the terrible condition of Germany, it was important for the Nazis to be seen to have played no part in the discredited republican governments.

People voted for the Nazis for three main reasons:

1 They were anxious about the economy.
2 They were nervous about the rise of Communism.
3 They felt the Weimar parties had failed.

Hitler was a gifted public speaker. He captivated audiences and played on their fears and hopes. During election campaigns he spoke to thousands of Germans at hundreds of meetings. The strength of his personality gave a real sense of unity to the Party.

During the presidential elections of 1932, Goebbels hit upon the idea of using an aeroplane to enable Hitler to appear at a number of venues in the same day. The campaign was given the name 'Hitler over Germany'.

Goebbels carefully stage-managed impressive political rallies. They were on a huge scale with thousands of uniformed Nazis parading in massed ranks. Music, light shows and rousing speeches all added to the atmosphere. The Nazis gave the impression of order and discipline. During the chaos of the Depression years, many Germans felt reassured by this image of strength and unity.

In 1932 **Luise Solmitz**, a Hamburg schoolteacher, recorded her impressions of a Nazi rally:

'There was immaculate order and discipline....The hours passed, the sun shone, expectations rose....Testing of the loudspeakers, buzzing of the cine cameras. It was nearly 3 p.m. "The Führer is coming!" A ripple went through the crowds.... A speaker opened the meeting...nobody listened to him.... A second speaker welcomed Hitler and made way for the man who had drawn 120,000 people of all classes and ages. There stood Hitler in a simple black coat and looked over the crowd, waiting – a forest of swastika pennants swished up, the jubilation of this moment was given vent in a roaring salute. Main theme: out of parties shall grow a nation, the German nation.... When the speech was over there was roaring enthusiasm and applause.... Then he went. How many look up to him with touching faith! as their helper, their saviour, their deliverer from unbearable distress.'

Much of the Nazi vote came from the middle class and from rural workers. They had been badly hit by the economic collapse and particularly feared the rise of Communism which was making rapid progress in the depressed industrial cities. The army, big business, peasants and the middle class knew that they had much to lose if the Communists gained power. Nazi stormtroopers fought the Communists on the streets and claimed to be the only party defending the nation against the menace of Communism. The Weimar parties could not keep order. They were blamed for the economic crisis and they had lost the confidence of the people. The Nazis, with a promise and a solution for every problem, won votes because they appeared to offer hope to millions of bewildered Germans.

Caution! Some Nazi myths

Accounts of the Nazi rise to power sometimes confuse the facts. In the chart below are four common explanations for the success of the Nazis. Recent research shows how unreliable these interpretations are.

EXPLANATION	RECENT RESEARCH
1 After 1929 there was high unemployment in Germany. The unemployed turned to Hitler who promised them jobs.	Unemployed workers were mainly concentrated in the big industrial towns. This is where the Nazis did least well at election time. The unemployed were much more likely to vote for the Communists.
2 Germans regarded Hitler as a 'saviour'.	It's true that some Germans regarded Hitler as the answer to their prayers. However, the highest proportion of the popular vote won by the Nazis before Hitler came to power was just over 37 per cent (July 1932 elections). This meant that even at the height of their popularity, the Nazis were rejected by 63 per cent of voting Germans.
3 Money poured into Nazi funds from big business. This enabled the Party to finance massive election campaigns.	The Nazis did not need the contributions of leading industrialists. The Party was mostly self-funding. Some leaders of big business, such as Fritz Thyssen, did provide money but he was not typical of other businessmen. Big business tended to make contributions to a range of parties as a kind of political insurance. Many leading businessmen distrusted the Nazis and found their liking for street violence and racism distasteful.
4 The Nazis won mass support by attacking the Jews.	Anti-Semitism was part of the Nazi creed and it was certainly evident in Nazi propaganda. However, it did not play a significant role in propaganda at election times and was not used as an issue around which people could be mobilised. It was more common to see people being roused by issues such as the Treaty of Versailles or the threat of Communism.

QUESTIONS

1 **Why were the Nazis unable to win much support in the years 1924–28?**

2 **Describe how each of the following factors helped the Nazis to win support after 1928:**

(a) **the Great Depression**

(b) **the Nazis' new political tactics**

3 **Why was Nazi propaganda so effective?**

4 **Look at the chart below. Which groups of Germans were attracted to the Party by these Nazi promises? Choose from the list below. Some promises appealed to more than one group.**

NAZI PROMISE	APPEALED TO:
1 Destroy the Treaty of Versailles and restore national pride.	
2 Prevent the rise of Communism.	
3 Reduce taxation.	
4 Provide jobs.	
5 Protect German agriculture, industry and small businesses from foreign competition.	
6 Build up the armed forces, expand German territory, restore Germany's importance in world affairs.	
7 Protect the purity of the German race against groups like the Jews.	
8 Curb the power of the Trade Unions.	

the army - leaders of industry - peasant farmers - the unemployed - the middle class
small businessmen - nationalists - racists

4 The Nazi Dictatorship

The road to dictatorship

When Hitler became Chancellor on 30 January 1933, his grip on Germany was not yet secure. His party did not have a majority in the Reichstag, he was one of only three Nazis in a Cabinet of twelve, and President Hindenburg had the power to dismiss his new Chancellor at any time. Yet in a matter of months, Hitler destroyed German democracy and set up a brutal dictatorship.

The first step along the road to dictatorship was taken with the calling of fresh elections. Hitler despised the moderate parties in the Reichstag and had no intention of working with them for any longer than he had to. He was convinced that another election would bring the Nazis a majority.

The following pages show how Germany was transformed into a dictatorship.

The trial for the Reichstag Fire, Leipzig 1933. Marinus van der Lubbe standing in the defendants' dock.

1933

30 January:
Hitler appointed Chancellor of Germany.

27 February:
The Reichstag Fire. The Reichstag building in Berlin was destroyed by fire. A Dutch Communist, Marinus van der Lubbe, was discovered at the scene and accused of arson. The Nazis presented the incident as the first stage of a Communist revolutionary plot. Overnight, 4000 Communist Party officials were arrested.

28 February:
Decree for the Protection of the People and the State. The Nazis persuaded President Hindenburg to pass this emergency law in the wake of the Reichstag Fire. The decree took away all basic rights from the German people including freedom of speech and assembly. It authorised phone taps and house searches. The Nazis exploited the new law in the final days before the Reichstag elections and made it next to impossible for their opponents to campaign freely.

5 March:
Election day. The Nazis won 288 seats, their best ever performance. However, they did not win an outright majority. They needed the 52 seats of the Nationalists to give them a 51.7 per cent majority. It was far from being the convincing result Hitler had hoped for.

23 March:
The Enabling Act. This Act destroyed parliamentary democracy. It gave Hitler the right to make his own laws without needing the approval of the Reichstag. The other political parties in Germany instantly lost their significance.

7 April:
A new law removed Jews and political opponents of the Nazis from their posts in the civil service.

2 May:
All independent trade unions were closed down. Their offices were occupied by Nazi Stormtroopers and their leaders arrested. Many were sent to the new concentration camps which had been set up in February. All workers now became part of a huge official 'trade union' called the

German Labour Front. This was a Nazi organisation led by Robert Ley.

26 May:
The Communist Party was banned.

22 June:
The Social Democratic Party was banned.

5 July:
The Catholic Centre Party closed itself down following an agreement between the Nazi government and the Vatican. The Church agreed that no Catholic political party should operate in Germany in return for a Nazi assurance that the Church could carry on its religious work without interference.

14 July:
Law against the Formation of Parties. This law declared that the Nazis were the only legal political party in Germany. Anyone attempting to set up, or run, a rival political party would be jailed. In December Hitler announced that there was no difference between the Party and the State. Nazi organisations like the SS became part of the official government.

1934

Ernst Rohm

30 January:

The state parliaments representing the regions of Germany were abolished.

30 June:

The Night of the Long Knives. By 1934, the SA had become enormously powerful with more than two million members. Its leader, Ernst Rohm, had particular ideas about the direction he thought the Nazis should be taking. In particular, Rohm wanted Hitler to merge the regular army with his own stormtroopers and place them under his command. He also urged Hitler to adopt more socialist policies and to act against industrialists and big business. Hitler rejected these ideas and was persuaded by Goebbels that Rohm was plotting against him. He acted swiftly against the 'threat' of the SA. In the early hours of 30 June, Rohm and other SA leaders were dragged from their beds by squads of SS men. Within hours of their arrest, they were dead. Rohm, after refusing to commit suicide in his prison cell, was shot in the head by an SS officer. The power of the SA had been brutally destroyed.

2 August:

President Hindenburg died. Hitler announced that there would be no presidential election. He united the offices of President and Chancellor and took responsibility for both. Hitler was now known simply as Führer (leader) of Germany. On the same day, the army swore a personal oath of loyalty to Hitler. Army leaders were grateful to Hitler for saving them from Rohm and the SA.

> *'I swear to God this holy oath that I shall offer total obedience to the Führer of the German Reich and people, Adolf Hitler, the supreme commander of the Army, and that I shall be prepared, as a brave soldier, to lay down my life at any time.'*

The role of Goering

Hermann Goering (left) was a leading Nazi and member of the Cabinet. As Minister of the Interior for Prussia he had control of the police and administration in three-fifths of Germany. From this position, he took the lead against the Nazis' opponents. He organised a purge of Prussian police chiefs, removing all non-Nazis. He also brought in 40,000 SA and SS men to serve as auxiliary police officers. They were given arm-bands and guns, and explicit instructions from Goering on how to use them:

'Communist terrorist acts and attacks are to be proceeded against with all severity, and weapons must be used ruthlessly when necessary. Police officers, who in the execution of this duty use their firearms, will be supported by me without regard to the effect of their shots; on the other hand, officers who fail from a false sense of consideration may expect disciplinary measures.'

Goering's actions removed the protection of the regular police force and made it quite impossible for other parties to campaign freely in large parts of Germany.

The strategy of terror

Terror and intimidation were vital ingredients in the making of the Nazi dictatorship. During the election campaign of February 1933, over 50 Nazi opponents were killed in street violence. Stormtroopers disrupted the meetings of political opponents and individuals suffered terrible beatings.

This Socialist decided to stop making public speeches after his meetings had been hijacked by Stormtroopers:

> '*Several of my meetings have been disrupted and a considerable section of the audience had to be taken away badly injured.... I therefore request the cancellation of meetings with me as speaker. As things are, there is obviously no longer any police protection sufficient to check the aggressive actions of the SA and SS at my meetings.*'

Grzesinski, former SPD Police President in Berlin, 24 February 1933.

The Nazis were ruthless in eliminating opponents. Mass arrests and removal to concentration camps was the favoured method. It wasn't just political opponents like Communists and Social Democrats who were targeted. The Nazi security police had orders to arrest all kinds of people including Jews, freemasons, trade unionists, common criminals, traitors, abortionists and homosexuals. Even people

who dared to complain about the Nazis were taken out of circulation. The Nazis created an atmosphere of fear where a careless word or a strongly-held opinion could result in a beating, arrest or even death.

The suffering of the Jews began as soon as the Nazis came to power. They were assaulted and terrorised on the streets by racist Stormtroopers. On 1 April 1933, a boycott of Jewish shops began. People who bought goods from Jewish shopkeepers or who visited a Jewish doctor were accused of being traitors. SA men took up position outside Jewish businesses to enforce the boycott.

Nazi guard in front of a boycotted Jewish shop in Berlin 1933.

Nazis arresting political opponents in 1933.

A member of the Gestapo going over suspects for concealed weapons, while his companion covers the men with a pistol.

Heinrich Himmler

Hitler inspecting SS Guards.

QUESTIONS

1 How effective was Nazi control over Germany at the end of January 1933?

2 Why did Hitler call for new elections soon after becoming Chancellor?

3 What was significant about the timing of the Reichstag Fire?

4 What was the importance of Hermann Goering in establishing the Nazi dictatorship?

5 The list below contains some of the features commonly found in dictatorships.

  * an emphasis on one supreme leader

  * a close partnership with the armed forces

  * the making of laws without reference to parliament

  * the banning of independent organisations such as trade unions

  * the removal of basic rights such as freedom of speech

  * the use of terror and intimidation to silence opposition and keep control

  * a single state political party – all other parties banned

Using this framework, and the information on pages 34–39, explain why Germany could be described as a dictatorship by August 1934.

Much of Hitler's terror strategy relied on the SS. This elite force had been set up in 1925 as a bodyguard for Hitler and other Nazi leaders. In 1929, Heinrich Himmler took control of the SS. He separated it from the SA and expanded its membership. SS men were given sinister black uniforms and a new role as the Nazi Party's security police. The SS developed specialist units including the **Death's Head Guards**, who operated the concentration camps, and the **Gestapo**, which hunted down 'enemies of the State'. The SS were absolutely loyal to Hitler and showed no mercy in carrying out their duties, as SA leaders discovered during the Night of the Long Knives.

The Reichstag Fire – the work of the Communists?

SOURCE A

'I must insist that my action was inspired by political motives…. As to the question whether I acted alone, I declare emphatically that this was the case. No one at all helped me.'

Van der Lubbe in a statement to the police, 3 March 1933.

SOURCE B

'The burning has long been credited to Goering. Indeed, all the evidence pointed in this direction. There was an underground tunnel from his office to the Reichstag giving him ample opportunity to send his agents into the building unobserved. His behaviour when he arrived on the scene, was such as to attract the utmost attention. He was clearly enjoying himself. A Dutchman, Lubbe, was found wandering in the building and claimed to have set fire to the Reichstag but since he was three-quarters blind, quite mad and incapable of any co-ordinated movements, the claim could not be taken seriously.'

Robert Payne, *The Life and Death of Adolf Hitler* (1973). Payne is a British historian.

SOURCE C

'Goering seems to have been utterly thunderstruck; he went at once to the burning building. His first thought was to save the tapestries and the library… It cannot be inferred from Goering's behaviour that he welcomed the fire.'

Hans Mommsen, *Aspects of the Third Reich* (1985). Mommsen is a German historian.

SOURCE D

'Hitler's election prospects were not good. The disillusionment of the masses would show itself on 5 March in an increased Communist vote. It became a necessity to change the situation by some act of provocation….Then the elections could be carried out when violent feeling against the Communists and Socialists was at its height.'

Extract from *The Brown Book of the Hitler Terror* (1933). This book was published through the Communist International Propaganda Organisation based in Paris.

QUESTIONS

1 **According to Source D, who was responsible for the Reichstag Fire? How reliable do you consider this explanation to be?**

2 **Study Source A. How useful is this source to an historian studying the Reichstag Fire?**

3 **Study sources B and C. Payne and Mommsen are both historians but they appear to disagree about Goering's role in the Reichstag Fire. Why do you think their interpretations are so different?**

4 **'Van der Lubbe set fire to the Reichstag as part of a Communist plot.' Do you agree or disagree with this claim? Use all the sources to help explain your answer.**

The Night of the Long Knives

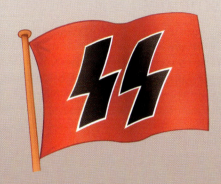

SOURCE A

'I note from the reports I have received that through your decisive intervention and your courageous personal commitment you have nipped all the treasonable intrigues in the bud. You have saved the German nation from serious danger and for this I express to you my deeply felt gratitude and my sincere appreciation.'

President von Hindenburg in an official telegram to Hitler, 2 July 1934. By this time, the President was hopelessly senile and had only one month to live.

SOURCE B

'After the month of May, there could be no further doubt that the Chief-of-Staff, Rohm, was busied with ambitious schemes which, if realised, could only lead to the most violent disturbances....The preparations made for the revolt were very extensive....Only ruthless and bloody intervention could prevent the revolution from spreading.'

Part of Hitler's speech to the Reichstag justifying his actions, 13 July 1934.

SOURCE C

'Among [the SA] there were soon mutterings about a "second revolution", not to be directed against Hitler, but against the conservatives...who surrounded him. The army began to take military precautions which were reciprocated by the SA. Tension increased visibly in the course of June 1934, but it is certain that Rohm did not prepare a putsch. He sent his men on leave and retired to his house at Wiessee in Bavaria where he expected a visit from Hitler. But Rohm's opponents, above all Himmler, the leader of the SS, and some army leaders, succeeded in convincing Hitler that he was planning a putsch. Hitler decided to side with the stronger battalions and against his old friend and protector...'

F. L. Carsten, *The Rise of Fascism* (1967).

SOURCE D

'Haven't I worked hard all my life for this land, and given Hitler all I had. Where would he be without me? Hitler had better look out – the German revolution is only beginning... if he thinks he can squeeze me for his own ends for ever, and some fine day throw me on the ash heap, he's wrong. The SA can also be an instrument for checking Hitler.'

Rohm allegedly made these comments to one of Hitler's henchmen, Kurt Ludecke in June 1933. Ludecke published his version of events in a book *I knew Hitler* in 1938.

QUESTIONS

1 In Source A, President Hindenburg appears to accept that the SA were involved in a 'treasonable' plot. Does this prove that such a plot existed?

2 Study Sources B and C. Carsten and Hitler give different explanations for the events of 30 June 1934. Why do you think these interpretations are so different?

3 'The Night of the Long Knives was necessary because Rohm planned to seize power in Germany by force.' Do you agree or disagree with this claim? Use all the sources to help explain your answer.

5 Living in the Third Reich

The Nazi economy

When Hitler took power in 1933, the German economy was in tatters. His greatest short-term challenge, therefore, was to restore confidence and get people back to work. If Hitler failed to deliver his election promises, his credibility with the German people would be lost. During the years 1933–39, the economy did indeed improve and the Nazis were quick to claim the credit for the transformation.

ASSIGNMENT

This section allows you to investigate the recovery and the impact of Nazi economic policies on the German people. Use the data contained on these pages to respond to the following questions:

1 How genuine was the fall in unemployment in 1933–39?

2 Did all Germans benefit from Nazi economic policies?

3 Was Germany's recovery only due to Nazi economic policies?

1 German unemployment 1933–39

Year	Number of unemployed	% of total work force unemployed
1933	6,014,000	25.9
1934	3,773,000	13.5
1935	2,974,000	10.3
1936	2,520,000	7.4
1937	1,853,000	4.1
1938	1,052,000	1.9
1939	302,000	0.5

2 Job creation schemes

Since Hitler had been a constant critic of the Weimar's unemployment crisis, it was essential for him to quickly get people back to work. Initially, the Nazis did this by spending vast sums of public money on job creation schemes. Public spending under the Nazis increased dramatically, as the table below shows.

Year	Amount in billions of marks
1933	18.4
1934	21.6
1938	37.1

The Nazis subsidised private firms, especially in the construction industry, to stimulate the economy. They also embarked on an ambitious road-building programme designed to provide Germany with 7000 km of motorways (autobahnen). In addition, new jobs were created within the growing ranks of the Nazi bureaucracy.

Men at work on an autobahn in the Alps.

3 Working hours

Average working hours in industry (per week)	
1933	42.9
1939	47.0

4 Production

The output of heavy industry increased dramatically in 1933–39.

- Coal and chemicals doubled.
- Oil, iron and steel trebled.
- Iron ore extraction increased five-fold.

The production of consumer goods increased at a much slower rate:

- Capital goods increased by approximately 150 per cent.
- Consumer goods increased by approximately 25 per cent.

5 Invisible unemployment

The official unemployment figures did not include the following groups:

- Jews dismissed from their jobs.
- Unmarried men under 25 who were pushed into National Labour Service schemes.
- Women dismissed from their jobs or tempted by the offer of State-marriage loans to give up work and get married.
- Opponents of the Nazi regime held in concentration camps.

The official figures were also distorted by the fact that:

- Part-time workers were counted as fully employed.
- The re-introduction of conscription in 1935 took thousands of young men into military service.

6 Trade Unions

Independent trade unions were amongst the first victims of the Nazi dictatorship. The unions were outlawed, their funds confiscated and their leaders arrested. The unions were replaced by the **German Labour Front** (Deutsche Arbeitsfront or DAF) under Dr Robert Ley.

Without the protection of independent trade unions, German workers were unable to negotiate wage rates or to take strike action. The Nazis made strikes illegal and abolished laws governing minimum wages and maximum working hours.

The movement of workers was regulated and government permission was needed to change jobs. Only State-operated labour exchanges could arrange new jobs for workers who wished to move.

7 National Labour Service

The **Reichsarbeitsdienst** or, RAD, put young men to work on public works schemes such as land reclamation, tree planting, construction and road-building. In July 1935, the Reich Labour Service Law made it compulsory for all German men between the ages of 18 and 25 to do six months training in the RAD. The National Labour Service succeeded in removing thousands of young men from the official unemployment figures but it was never very popular. The pocket-money wages were no substitute for a real pay packet and the uncomfortable tented camps offered no solution to the long-term problem of homelessness.

National Labour Service was not a Nazi invention. It was actually started towards the end of the Weimar Republic by political and youth groups as a way of giving the unemployed some useful purpose.

Robert Ley (centre) in 1939.

8 'Strength through Joy'

The 'Strength through Joy' organisation (Kraft durch Freude – KdF) was part of the German Labour Front. The KdF attempted to make the leisure time of German workers as purposeful and rewarding as possible. It was hoped that this would result in happy workers who would be better motivated to serve the Reich. The KdF sponsored a wide range of leisure and cultural activities including concerts, theatre visits, museum tours, sporting events, weekend trips, adult education courses, holidays and cruises. All were provided at low cost giving ordinary workers access to activities previously reserved for the better-off. However, very few workers were able either to afford or to secure places on showcase KdF activities such as cruises to Madeira and Scandinavia.

The 'Beauty of Work' department of the KdF had some success in improving working conditions. It organised the building of canteens, swimming pools and sports facilities and installed better lighting. Workers were expected to make these improvements themselves in their spare time, however, and without pay. Considerable resentment resulted from this scheme.

9 Rearmament

From the beginning, the Nazi economy was dominated by Hitler's obsession with Germany's military strength. A great deal of the work created in the Third Reich was associated with rearmament and military expansion.

Military expenditure 1933–38

Year	Amount in billions of marks	% of Net Domestic Product
1933	3.5	6.3
1938	26.0	38.1

The army grew from 100,000 men in 1933 to 1,400,000 in 1939.

Billions were spent producing military hardware such as tanks, ships and aircraft.

10 The cost of living

The cost of living increased during the 1930s. All basic groceries, with the exception of fish, cost more in 1939 than they had in 1933. Food items were in short supply partly because it was government policy to discourage agricultural production in order to keep up prices for the benefit of farmers.

11 The Volkswagen swindle

As part of the 'Strength through Joy' movement, Hitler wanted car ownership to expand. A new car, the Volkswagen (meaning 'people's car') was designed and, in 1938, Hitler laid the foundation stone for the factory in which it would be built. The car was to be cheap enough for the average family to afford. Ley persuaded large numbers of German workers to begin paying for a car on hire purchase before the VW factory began production. By the time war broke out in September 1939 however, not a single customer had taken delivery of a car. The factory was converted for war production and none of the money that the workers had paid in advance was refunded.

12 Progress before 1933

Before Hitler became Chancellor in January 1933, the German economy was beginning to pick up. The worst of the Depression was over and unemployment was falling. The improvement in the German economy under Hitler coincided with a general world economic recovery.

Under the last Weimar, Chancellors' (Bruning, Papen and Schleicher) job creation schemes had been established, but they were hindered by inadequate funding. The construction of the autobahn network, one of Hitler's most publicised achievements, was planned before Hitler took office. Indeed, public spending on road construction in 1934 was actually lower than it had been in 1927.

13 Autarky

In addition to reducing unemployment and rearming, a third objective of Nazi economic policy was to bring about 'autarky' – economic self-sufficiency. Hitler believed that Germany was too dependent on foreign imports and wanted to eliminate the need for them. As a result, the development and production of 'ersatz' materials was ordered. These were artificial substitutes for products such as oil, rubber, textiles and even food.

By 1939, the policy proved to have been a failure. Germany continued to import 33 per cent of its raw materials and 17 per cent of its food. Ersatz products were generally inferior and contributed to the declining living standards of German citizens.

14 Wages

Under the Nazis, local and national wage rates were scrapped. Wages were paid according to the 'performance principle'. The more work a person did, the more they were paid. Payment by this method suited the young and healthy but worked against the interests of older, less productive workers.

Between 1936 and 1939 the real value of take-home pay increased, but most of this gain was due to longer working days rather than a significant increase in hourly wage rates. People earned more because they worked harder and for longer periods of time. Work-related sickness and absenteeism increased as a result.

Controlling the people

The Nazis controlled the German people through a blend of persuasion and terror. Propaganda and indoctrination forced the people to conform to Nazi thinking, while the fear of arrest and the concentration camp kept active opposition to the regime to a minimum.

Persuasion: Propaganda

The Nazis made extensive use of propaganda during the 1930s. It was an important element in the Nazi rise to power (see Chapter 3) and its full power was harnessed after 1933 to ensure that Hitler stayed in control. To the Nazis, everything had propaganda value. Poster campaigns and mass rallies were tried and trusted methods of persuasion, but new technology such as the radio and the cinema was also utilised to shape and control public opinion. The press was dominated by the Nazis, as was every aspect of cultural expression including art, literature and music.

The Nazi propaganda message was designed to appeal to the masses. Ideas were kept simple and were repeated time and time again. Propaganda was made visually impressive through ritual and display. The great rallies at Nuremburg were masterpieces of stage-managed propaganda.

The Power of Radio

'Through technical devices like the radio…80 million people were deprived of independent thought. It was thereby possible to subject them to the will of one man.'

Albert Speer

Goebbels was quick to see the propaganda potential of radio. In March 1933, he told the controllers of German radio: 'I consider radio to be the most modern and the most crucial instrument that exists for influencing the masses.' He ordered manufacturers to mass produce cheap sets which even the poorest families could afford. By 1939, 70 per cent of German homes had a radio – the highest percentage of radio ownership in the world. Goebbels used the airwaves to broadcast the Nazi message directly into people's homes. He also encouraged community radio listening in factories, shops and offices and in cafés and bars. From 1938, loudspeaker systems were erected on the streets in dozens of cities to relay important Nazi events and messages.

Cinema

Goebbels had a personal interest in the cinema and created a special section within his Propaganda Ministry to supervise German film-makers. Scripts, performers and film production were monitored for quality and to ensure Nazi values were not offended. The Nazis produced about 1300 films during their time in power, but surprisingly only about 200 were direct propaganda. Goebbels understood that the German people would not accept too many obviously political films. He wanted the cinemas to be full so that when he had an important message the audiences would be present to hear it. People wanted to be entertained when they visited the cinema and Goebbels produced high quality films to achieve this. However, Nazi themes such as national sacrifice, anti-Semitism and Aryan heroism did underpin many of these films. All film performances were accompanied by a 45-minute official newsreel which glorified Hitler and Germany and publicised Nazi achievements.

An anti-Jewish poster entitled 'The Eternal Jew'.

Propaganda Showcase: The Berlin Olympics

In 1936 the Nazis staged the Olympic Games in Berlin. Everything about the games was designed to impress the outside world. The Olympic stadium was the largest in the world and could hold 110,000 spectators. Every detail was carefully stage-managed and news reports were controlled. Filming of the events came under the direction of Leni Riefenstahl. All camera crews had to be approved by her and all shots supervised. Her own film, *Olympia*, was the only official record of the games permitted and it was distributed world-wide.

For the duration of the games, the Nazi State wore a mask of respectability. Signs declaring 'Jews not wanted' were removed from public places and thousands of foreign visitors went away with a positive image of the new Germany. The supreme athlete of the games was the black American, Jesse Owens. His four gold medals made a mockery of Hitler's theory of Aryan superiority. Hitler could not hide his anger and refused to shake hands with Owens.

'Hitler was highly annoyed by the success of the black American runner, Jesse Owens. Hitler said that such people had an unfair advantage over civilised white people as they were descended from jungle primitives. They were unfair competition and would be excluded from future games.'

Albert Speer, *Inside the Third Reich.*

Culture

All forms of cultural expression including literature, theatre, art, music and film came under the control of the Propaganda Ministry. A special division of the Ministry, the Reich Chamber of Culture, was created in September 1933 to monitor cultural activities. All professional artists, whether they were musicians, actors or writers had to be members of the Chamber of Culture. Membership was only granted to those whose work was approved by the Nazis. Those denied membership found it impossible to get their work published or performed in Germany.

The Nazis had strong objections to certain types of artistic expression. They despised modern art and progressive theatre and regarded jazz music as evil. Jewish, Socialist and liberal artists were forced to leave Germany or stop working. As a result, Germany lost many of its most gifted authors, musicians, artists and film-makers. The Nazis saw artistic expression as a vehicle for promoting their ideas and educating the public. They encouraged artists to incorporate 'Aryan themes' such as national community, heroism, family and the glories of war into their work.

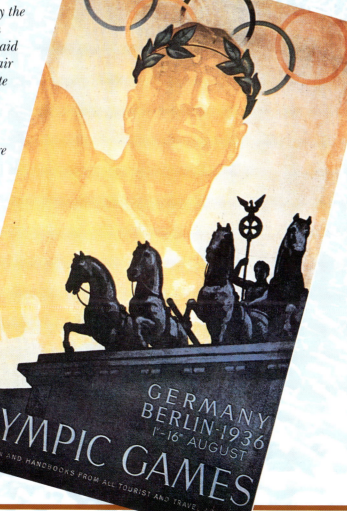

GERMANY BERLIN 1936 1ˢᵗ~16ᵗʰ AUGUST

OLYMPIC GAMES

INFORMATION AND HANDBOOKS FROM ALL TOURIST AND TRAVEL AGENCIES

Terror: The Police State

The SS and the Gestapo were the backbone of Hitler's police state. He used these loyal and ruthless Nazis to silence opposition and ensure conformity. The Gestapo (Geheime Staatspolizei) was the Secret State Police during the Third Reich. The Gestapo acted as 'thought police', hunting down and arresting political opponents. This sinister and much-feared organisation was set up in Prussia by Hermann Goering in 1933. Gestapo officers also had the power of 'protective arrest'. This meant that they could take people into custody merely on the suspicion that they were opposed to the Nazi State. Victims of the Gestapo were usually removed to concentration camps. In 1936 Heinrich Himmler assumed overall command of Germany's police forces, including the Gestapo.

The secret police maintained a vast network of informers and used them to carry out constant surveillance on the general public. Informers operated in every factory, office, school and apartment block. Even children were recruited to report the views of their parents to the Gestapo. Jokes against the Nazi State were dangerous. The penalty for telling a joke at Hitler's expense was death. The Germans were terrified into conformity in every respect. Even traditional greetings were replaced with the Nazi greeting 'Heil Hitler'. (For details on the SS, see Chapter 4.)

Concentration Camps

The Nazis built concentration camps soon after taking power in January 1933. The first were opened at Oranienburg, near Berlin and Dachau, in Bavaria. They were designed as secure prisons for political opponents and 'undesirables' and were run by the SS. Communists and trade union leaders were amongst the first inmates to experience the regime of hard labour and military-style discipline. Other groups who failed to conform to Nazi ideals including homosexuals, pacifists, vagrants and Jehovah's Witnesses were also imprisoned in the camp network. Although the camps were brutal places and deaths did occur behind the barbed wire there were, as yet, no gas chambers and crematoria, features which characterised the death camps of the 1940s. By 1939 there were only 25,000 prisoners held in the camps, a relatively small number compared to the hundreds of thousands who would live and die in them during the 1940s.

Censorship

The Nazis controlled all forms of media including newspapers, radio broadcasting, cinema, publishing, theatre and art. Strict censorship was applied to all material intended for a public audience. German radio was brought under State control in 1934 with the creation of the Reich Radio Company and all broadcasts were vetted by the Propaganda Ministry. The only news source which journalists were

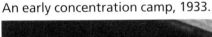
An early concentration camp, 1933.

Nazis and students throw black-listed literature into the fire.

authorised to use was the DNB, the State-controlled press agency. Detailed instructions for the treatment of the news were issued at daily press conferences organised by the Propaganda Ministry. Newspapers which printed unauthorised material or which presented the Nazi press with serious competition, were closed down. By 1939 Max Amann, the Nazi Press Chief, had direct control over two-thirds of Germany's daily newspapers.

The Nazis also applied a more direct form of censorship. In May 1933 they destroyed thousands of books in huge bonfires and later used the same tactic with works of art. However, it was 1936 before the Nazis produced an official list of banned books. By 1939 the list contained the names of 576 authors variously labelled as 'traitors', Communists and 'pornographers'.

The Churches

In the Church, the Nazis had a powerful rival for control of the hearts and minds of the German people. Some sections of the Church, including the Lutherans, supported Nazi ideals by choice. The so-called 'German Christians', a group within the Protestant Church, gave their full backing to the regime and were nicknamed the 'SA of the Church'. In general, however, the Church chose neither to criticise nor endorse the policies of the Nazis. This was not true of the Confessional Church which

openly attacked the Nazi regime. Its leader, Martin Niemöller, was arrested in 1937 along with hundreds of his supporters and was sent to Dachau where he remained until 1945.

In 1933 Hitler made an agreement with the Catholic Church known as the **Concordat**. Hitler promised that the Church could operate in Germany without interference and, in return, the Pope agreed to keep the Catholic Church out of politics. The Catholic authorities in Germany spent the next six years trying to hold on to their privileges as the Nazis attempted to undermine them. In southern Germany where the Catholic faith was very strong, there was active resistance to the Nazis. The arrest of priests and the closure of Catholic youth clubs provoked demonstrations and acts of civil disobedience. When the Nazis tried to have crucifixes removed from school classrooms, the outcry was so strong that the Nazis were forced to back down and replace them.

One religious group, the Jehovah's Witnesses, refused to submit to Hitler or compromise their beliefs in any way. In 1934 and 1935 they were arrested in large numbers and taken to concentration camps.

Although propaganda and terror brought stability to the Third Reich, few Germans were ever converted into committed Nazis. It is, of course, impossible to know the thoughts of private individuals, but even though the majority of people did not actively oppose the regime it does not mean that they had all become Nazis. People conformed because resistance was futile and dangerous.

It is also true that many Nazi policies reflected the values of millions of Germans and met with their approval. The ability of the Nazis to meet the basic needs of the people meant that there was a great deal of popular support for the government. Hitler's foreign policy successes after 1936 also contributed to the genuine enthusiasm for the regime.

QUESTIONS

1 **Why did the Nazis take control of radio broadcasting, newspapers and the cinema?**

2 **Describe the range of methods used by the Nazis to control the German people.**

3 **Why did the churches pose a major challenge to the authority of the Nazis?**

4 **What were the main themes of Nazi propaganda?**

Women, the family and racial policy

'The mission of women is to be beautiful and to bring children into the world'

Josef Goebbels, 1929.

The Nazis emphasised the differences between men and women and believed that nature had created each for different purposes. Men were responsible for decision-making and providing protection. Women were to bear children and ensure the domestic comfort of their families. They were expected to be dependent on men and to be obedient to their husbands. The Nazi slogan '*Kinder, Kirche, Kuche*' (Children, Church and Cooking) summed up what Nazis believed were the concerns of women.

To the Nazis, the ideal German woman was blonde, blue-eyed and sturdily built. She was expected to have broad hips for child-bearing and to have no interest in such things as fashion, make up and slimming.

1

Nazi 'Lonely Heart'

52-year-old pure Aryan physician, fighter at Tannenburg, wishing to settle down, desires male offspring through civil marriage with YOUNG, HEALTHY VIRGIN OF PURE ARYAN STOCK, UNDEMANDING, SUITED TO HEAVY WORK AND THRIFTY WITH FLAT HEELS, WITHOUT EARRINGS, IF POSSIBLE WITHOUT MONEY.

German marriage advertisement 1935.

Translation: Join the youth associations of the NS (Nazi Socialist) league and the German Women's associations.

Nazi policies

Nazi policy towards women and the family was based on two fears. Firstly, the fear that the German population was growing too slowly, making Germany vulnerable to its faster-breeding neighbours, particularly Poland and Russia. Secondly, the fear that the German people were becoming racially impure due to intermarriage with 'inferior' groups like the Jews and the Slavs. The Nazis, therefore, made it their policy to encourage more births and to prevent racial mixing.

From 1933 women were encouraged to give up their jobs, get married and have large families. Women in the professions such as medicine, the law, teaching and the civil service were targeted first and many were forced out of their jobs. Generous social security benefits and interest-free marriage loans were offered as incentives to women to stay at home

Translation: Support the Mother and Child Benefit.

and raise families. Couples could clear their marriage loan by having children. Each time a child was born the loan was cut by a quarter. By 1939, 42 per cent of all marriages were loan assisted. Hitler argued that a woman's intellect was of no importance to the Nazi State and places for women in higher education were cut.

A number of strategies were used to encourage more births.

- Laws against abortion were strictly enforced. Between 1934 and 1938 the conviction rate for crimes associated with abortion rose by 50 per cent.
- Birth-control clinics were closed down and access to contraceptive advice and devices was severely restricted.
- A massive propaganda campaign was launched to raise the status of housewives and mothers in society.
- The most productive mothers were awarded special medals at a ceremony held every year on the birthday of Hitler's mother.

2 The Nazis established 'Advice Centres for the Improvement of Genetic and Racial Health' where engaged couples could be given advice about marriage and having children. In 1934 the following 'Ten Commandments for the Choice of a Spouse' were issued:

1 Remember that you are a German.

2 If you are genetically healthy you should not remain unmarried.

3 Keep your body pure.

4 You should keep your mind and spirit pure.

5 As a German, choose only a spouse of the same or Nordic blood.

6 In choosing a spouse, ask about his ancestors.

7 Health is also a precondition for physical beauty.

8 Marry only for love.

9 Don't look for a playmate but for a companion for marriage.

10 You should want to have as many children as possible.

Quoted in Noakes and Pridham, *Nazism 1919-1945*, Vol. 2.

From 1936 the Nazis opened special maternity homes called **Lebensborn**. These were designed to be breeding centres for the production of pure Aryan children. Racially approved Aryan mothers were matched with SS fathers in a sinister experiment to replenish the Reich with pure bred German children.

How Successful were these Policies?

Between 1933 and 1939, the number of marriages increased and there was a sharp rise in the birth-rate in Germany. Yet these increases cannot be linked to Nazi population policy with any certainty. Other factors, such as the economic recovery in the inter-war years, may also have contributed. Also, despite the sharp rise in the birth-rate, it remained below the level recorded during the years 1922–26. It is also the case that the number of divorces rose during the Thirties.

In some respects, Nazi policies acted against the interests of the family. The shortage of affordable housing and resulting high rents created by the priority given to rearmament, meant that couples found it difficult to find accommodation suitable for having a large family. In addition, Labour Service and conscription made it less likely that young men would be able to marry and have children.

In 1933 there were 4.85 million women in paid employment. This increased to 7.14 million by 1939. Economic reality forced Nazi ideology to do a U-turn. A labour shortage began to develop from 1936 and the government looked to women to plug the gaps. In 1937 the Nazis overturned a clause in their marriage loans scheme to permit married women who had a loan, to take up employment. This reversed policy, however, was not very successful. The number of women in employment rose but remained behind the levels of the 1920s, despite the fact that there were two million more women of working age in 1939 than there had been in 1928.

Racial Hygiene

The Nazis were very interested in a branch of science known as **Eugenics** which aimed to develop techniques for racial improvement. Hitler ordered measures to ensure that 'undesirables' did not have children. He restricted welfare support and marriage loans to Aryan Germans – Jews and other non-Aryans were not eligible at all. Political opponents and people with physical disabilities or mental illness were also denied these benefits.

In July 1933, the Nazis passed the Law for the Prevention of Hereditarily Diseased Offspring. This made sterilisation compulsory for people suffering from hereditary illness or who had physical disabilities. The list included people with depression, epilepsy, blindness, deafness, the physically handicapped and alcoholics. By 1937 almost 200,000 compulsory sterilisations had been performed (102,218 men, 95,165 women).

3

The following were the reasons the Nazis gave for the introduction of the sterilisation law:

'...public opinion has become increasingly preoccupied with questions of population policy and the continuing decline in the birth-rate. However, it is not only the decline in population which is the cause of serious concern but equally the increasingly evident genetic make-up of our people. Whereas the hereditarily healthy families have for the most part adopted a policy of having only one or two children, countless numbers of inferiors and those suffering from hereditary ailments are reproducing unrestrainedly while their sick and asocial offspring are a burden on the community...'

Quoted in Noakes and Pridham, *Nazism 1919-45*, Vol. 2.

Further legislation in 1935 placed restrictions on marriage itself. In September, the Law for the Protection of German Blood and German Honour banned marriages between Jews and German citizens. Sexual relations between Jews and Germans were also forbidden. One month later, the Law for the Protection of the Hereditary Health of the German People (Marriage Health Law) was passed by the Nazis. This introduced a ban on the marriage of people with infectious or hereditary illnesses.

QUESTIONS

1 **What methods did the Nazis use to try to increase the population of Germany?**

2 **Why did the Nazis want the population to expand?**

3 **How successful were Nazi policies towards women and the family?**

4 **Which groups in German society suffered as a result of Nazi population policies?**

The place of women in Nazi Germany

SOURCE C

'Within months of Hitler coming to power, many women doctors and civil servants were sacked from their jobs. Then women lawyers and teachers were dismissed. By 1939 there were few women left in professional jobs.'

Josh Brooman, *Hitler's Germany*, (1985).

SOURCE A

'German women wish in the main to be wives and mothers. They do not wish to be comrades.... They have no longing for the factory, no longing for the office. A cosy home, a loved husband and a multitude of happy children are closer to their hearts.'

Nazi Party pamphlet from the 1930s.

SOURCE D

'In 1933 almost 5 million women were in paid employment outside the home, whereas the figure had risen to 7.14 million by 1939. Labour shortage and rising wages thus drew many females into industrial employment, despite the regime's ideological goals.'

Dick Geary, *Nazism*, (1993).

SOURCE B

Employment of women in Germany (in millions).

	1933	1939
Agriculture and forestry	4.6	4.9
Industry and crafts	2.7	3.3
Trade and transport	1.9	2.1
Non-domestic services	0.9	1.1
Domestic service	1.2	1.3

QUESTIONS

1 How reliable is source A as evidence of women's attitudes in Nazi Germany?

2 How useful is source B to an historian studying the employment of women in Nazi Germany?

3 Sources C and D appear to give different impressions of the employment of women in Germany 1933-1939. How would you account for these different interpretations?

Hitler and the Jews

In 1933 there were almost half a million Jews living in Germany. Most had German citizenship and were proud of their nationality – 100,000 Jews had fought for Germany in the World War I. Jews lived and worked alongside their fellow Germans and made positive contributions to the economy. This hard-working and loyal minority, however, was despised by Hitler. Time after time he referred to the Jews as parasites and likened them to rats and germs.

> **1**
> *'Was there any form of filth or crime...without at least one Jew involved in it? If you cut continuously into such a sore, you find like a maggot in a rotting body, often dazzled by the sudden light – a Jew.'*
>
> Hitler, **Mein Kampf**, (1924).

This kind of vicious racism is known as **anti-Semitism**. It has a long tradition in European history and was part of the Nazi Party's programme as early as 1920.

> **2**
> *'Only members of the nation may be citizens of the State. Only those of German blood, regardless of religion, may be members of the nation. Thus, no Jew may be a member of the nation.'*
>
> The Nazi 25 Point Programme, 1920, quoted in Noakes and Pridham, *Nazism 1919–1945*, Vol. 1.

Hitler's racial ideas were set out in his book, *Mein Kampf*. He observed that the world was made up of different races and argued that they were not equal. He identified the 'Aryans' as the superior race, responsible for creating all civilisation. Although he failed to define what he meant by 'Aryan', it was clear that he felt the Germans to be of Aryan stock. He portrayed the Jews and other non-Aryans as inferior and less than human. He regarded the Jews as an evil force and was convinced of their involvement in a world conspiracy to destroy civilisation. Before and after taking power in Germany, Hitler used the Jews as scapegoats for all of society's problems. He blamed them for Germany's defeat in World War I and for the humiliation of the Versailles Treaty. He accused them of being the evil force behind Communism and of causing the Great Depression. In 1939, Hitler predicted that if another war broke out in Europe, it would be the fault of the Jews.

Hitler's hatred of the Jews developed into a clear objective. He wanted to eliminate the Jew from German society and to purify the Aryan race. He had no master-plan for achieving this, however, and until the beginning of World War II, a great deal of Nazi Jewish policy was unco-ordinated.

Nazi cartoon entitled 'Jewish department store octopus'.

The writing on this anti-Semitic beer mat says, 'Whoever buys from a Jew is a national traitor.'

Illustrations from a children's book, warning children not to trust Jews.

Cartoon from the Nazi newspaper Der Sturmer, 1935.

QUESTIONS

1 Why did the Nazis include anti-Jewish pictures in children's books?

2 What do these propaganda images accuse the Jews of being responsible for?

3 How would (a) the German people and (b) the Jews, have responded to such propaganda?

4 How useful is such propaganda to historians wishing to learn about the attitude of Germans to the Jews?

The persecution of the Jews

From the moment the Nazis took power, they began to persecute Germany's Jewish minority. Nazi policies were designed to isolate and exclude Jews from German society and to prevent racial intermixing. Jews were harassed and humiliated on the streets and were subjected to laws which robbed them of their rights, their livelihoods and their dignity.

1933

March: Sporadic and largely unplanned violence against Jews erupted in many towns and cities following the March elections. Much of this activity was organised by local SA commanders.

1 April: Nationwide boycott of Jewish shops and businesses. This action was ordered by Hitler and enforced by the SA.

7 April: The Law for the Restoration of a Professional Civil Service ordered the compulsory retirement of Jewish civil servants and the dismissal of Jewish workers employed in public service.

A Jew being forced to paint 'Jude' (Jew) on the wall of his father's shop.

10 May: Works by Jewish authors destroyed in Nazi organised book-burning sessions in Berlin.

22 September: Jews banned from all cultural activities by the Reich Chamber of Culture.
September: Farmers forced to prove that there had been no Jewish blood in their families since 1880 in order to be allowed to inherit land.

October: Jews excluded from journalism.

1934

Jewish students banned from taking professional exams in dentistry, medicine, law and pharmacy.

1935

21 May: Jews forbidden to join the German army. This ban was extended to all branches of the armed forces in July.

15 September: The Nuremburg Laws deprived Jews of German citizenship and made marriage and sexual relations between Germans and Jews illegal.

1936

March: Jews forbidden to run or lease a pharmacy

April: Jews forbidden to practise as vets.

October: Jewish teachers forbidden to give private tuition to German students.

The wrecked and pillaged windows of a Jewish shop, Berlin.

November: Jews forbidden to use the 'German' greeting 'Heil Hitler'.

1938

March: Anti-Jewish persecution extended to Nazi occupied Austria.

23 July: Jews issued with separate identity cards.

25 July: Jewish doctors restricted to treating other Jews only.

The placard on the right reads: 'As a Jewish boy I always take German girls up to my room'. The placard on the left reads: 'I am the biggest sow in town. I never on the Jew boys frown.'

17 August: Jews forced to adopt the specifically Jewish forenames of 'Sarah' and 'Israel'.

27 September: Jewish lawyers restricted to working for Jewish clients.

5 October: Jewish passports stamped with a 'J'.

Sept – Oct: 17,000 Polish Jews living in Germany rounded up by the SS and moved to the border with Poland.

9 November: Kristallnacht ('Night of the Broken Glass'). Nationwide pogrom (organised massacre) against Jewish communities following the murder by a Jew, of a Nazi official, Ernst von Rath in Paris. Ninety-one Jews were murdered, 191 synagogues destroyed and 7000 businesses wrecked. There was massive damage to Jewish property and Jewish cemetaries were desecrated. 30,000 Jews were arrested and taken to concentration camps where an estimated 2000 were murdered. Most of the destruction was carried out by the police and SA.

12 November: Jews fined one billion marks for the murder of von Rath and forbidden to attend places of entertainment.

15 November: Jewish children expelled form German schools.

3 December: The compulsory 'Aryanisation' of Jewish businesses was begun. This meant the compulsory sale of Jewish business property at ridiculously low prices.

1939

24 January: The Reich Central Office for Jewish Emigration was established with Reinhard Heydrich as its director.

21 February: Jews required to surrender precious metals and jewellery.

30 April: Jews evicted from their homes and forced into designated Jewish accommodation.

20 September: Jews forced to hand in their radio sets.

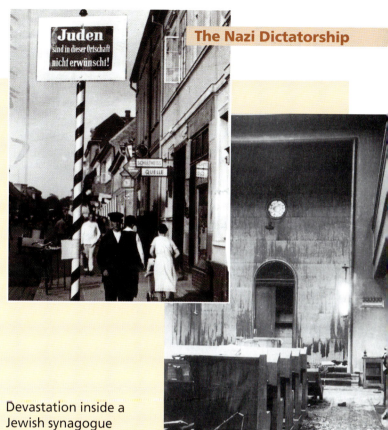

Devastation inside a Jewish synagogue following Kristallnacht.

1 Between 1933 and 1939 280,000 of Germany's half a million Jews emigrated.

2 Public signs made it clear that Jews were not welcome in places such as restaurants, sports stadiums, shops and cinemas. Many towns displayed such signs on main roads (see picture above). In the summer of 1936 these signs were removed for the duration of the Olympic Games in Berlin to avoid international criticism. Jewish-sounding street names were changed and Jewish names were erased from hundreds of war memorials.

Q U E S T I O N S

1 **How did Nazi policies towards the Jews affect:**

   (a) their ability to earn a living

   (b) their civil rights

   (c) their dignity and self-respect

2 **What was the purpose of these anti-Jewish measures?**

3 **Did Nazi policy towards the Jews change in the years 1920–1939?**

Youth

Hitler told the youth of Germany that they would one day inherit all he had created, so he placed great emphasis on preparing young people to be loyal and enthusiastic supporters of the Nazi State. To achieve this, he took control of the German youth movement and the schools.

Before the Nazis took power in 1933, almost six million young Germans were already organised into dozens of clubs and societies. This variety did not suit Hitler's purpose and, with the exception of church groups, he promptly banned them. Young people were now encouraged to join the **Hitler Youth**. This organisation had been set up in 1926 and, in July 1933, came under the control of the 'Youth Leader of the Reich', Baldur von Schirach. The pupose of Hitler Youth was made clear by Hitler in 1936:

> '*All German young people...will be educated in the Hitler Youth physically, intellectually and morally in the spirit of National Socialism [Nazism] to serve the nation and the community.*'

Hence Hitler Youth activities were based on competition, physical fitness and military training. Youth leaders organised hundreds of sporting contests and other activities such as hiking.

At their meetings, Hitler Youth members were made to parade and drill in military fashion and they were instructed in skills such as shooting, map reading

1

'*Pale-faced little fellows sometimes made a march of thirty miles, singing Nazi songs through the night, for their graduation from the Pimpfen ranks and acceptance into the Jungvolk. Some famous Nazi shrine is usually chosen as the scene of their graduation ceremony. The "bloodflag", one of the gory banners saved from the fighting days of the Party, a flag carried by a Nazi enthusiast who was killed by a Communist, always figures in these rituals. The boys raise their hands and make this solemn oath:*

"*In the presence of this bloodflag which represents out Führer, I swear to devote all my energies, all my strength, to the saviour of our country, Adolf Hitler. I am willing and ready to give up my life for him, so help me God. One People, One Nation, One Führer!*"'

Anna Rauschning, *No Retreat* (1943).

and signalling. There were also annual military-style camps which encouraged teamwork and comradeship. Through these activities, young people were taught the importance of 'Aryan qualities' such as obedience, self-sacrifice, discipline and endurance. There were also large helpings of political indoctrination. Formal lessons taught children about Aryan superiority, the nobility of war, the importance of the State and loyalty to Hitler. Nazi philosophy was also incorporated into the rituals and songs of the movement.

Girls were encouraged into the Nazi youth movement but they were kept strictly apart from the boys. They, too, were indoctrinated with Nazi ideas and were taught the same 'Aryan' ideals as the boys. However, the main emphasis of their experience in the Hitler Youth was on physical fitness and domestic skills. While the boys played with guns, the girls learned how to make beds and cook.

Translation: You also belong to the Führer!

Physical fitness was encouraged through sports, camps and marches, not as a preparation for military service, but in readiness for motherhood. Hitler Youth members were recruited as part of the Gestapo surveillance network. They were encouraged to monitor their parents, teachers and other adults and report them for disloyalty to the State.

The Nazi youth movement was part of a bigger strategy designed to control the lives of German citizens from the day they were born to the day they died:

'Our state…does not let a man go free from the cradle to the grave. We start our work when the child is three. As soon as it begins to think, a little flag is put into its hand. Then comes school, the Hitler Youth, the Storm Troopers and military training. We don't let a single soul go, and when all that is done there is the Labour Front, which takes possession of them when they are grown up and does not let them go until they die, whether they like it or not.'

Dr Robert Ley, leader of the Nazi Labour Front.

As a result, children as young as six were recruited into the youth movement.

2 Hitler Youth groups

Age	Boys	Girls
6-10	The Pimpfen (Little Fellows)	
10-14	The Jungvolk (Young Folk)	The Jungmadel (Young Girls)
14-18	Hitlerjugend (Hitler Youth)	The Bund Deutsche Madchen (the German Girls League)

How popular was the Hitler Youth movement?

Membership of the Hitler Youth was greatly expanded during the 1930s.

1932 - 108,000
1936 - 5.4 million
1939 - 8.0 million

In spite of these impressive figures it should be noted that more than three million young Germans had not joined the Hitler Youth by the beginning of 1938. In 1939 the authorities were forced to make membership of the Hitler Youth compulsory. The growth of the Hitler Youth movement was partly the result of negative pressures. The abolition of most other youth groups in 1933 left young people with few alternatives if they wanted to be involved in group activities such as sport. Government workers such as civil servants faced dismissal if their children were not members of the Hitler Youth. In 1936 church youth organisations were closed down (with the exception of Catholic clubs). Parents who prevented their children from joining the Hitler Youth could be fined and imprisoned. Later, the price for defiance could be much higher.

3 *'By their hostile attitude to the State these two parents have prevented their children from joining the Hitler Youth. The result is that the National Socialist [Nazi] education of these children is made to depend entirely on the school. But the school alone is not able to undo the strong influence of the parents… A father who keeps his children away from the Hitler Youth abuses his parental power. It will therefore be taken from him…'*

From **Peter F. Wiener**, *German with Tears* (1942)

Hitler with a young SA mascot.

By the end of the 1930s there is evidence that the movement was experiencing something of a crisis. A shortage of adult youth leaders resulted from military conscription and the decision of many teachers to withdraw their support for the movement. Teachers were becoming increasingly concerned about the effect Hitler Youth activities were having on student motivation, homework and discipline. Many parents were also worried about the effects on family life. They found it difficult to accept that the first loyalty of their children was to Hitler and they were concerned about the effects of so much propaganda on young minds. As children grew older, the spirit of independence which the Hitler Youth had given them often surfaced, causing them to challenge the views and authority of their parents. Some parents even became afraid of their children and worried that they might report them to the Gestapo.

Towards the end of the 1930s the Hitler Youth became increasingly concerned with military training. This, and the fact that the Nazis tried to prohibit certain activities, led some rebellious teenagers to remain outside the youth movement where they defied the Nazis. The banning of American swing and jazz music was resisted by some middle-class teenagers who organised parties where they could dance to the outlawed tunes. They mixed with Jews, had sex, dressed casually and earned the name 'Swing Youth'. Working-class teenagers in the cities formed gangs with names like the 'Raving Dudes' and the 'Navajos'. The Nazis identified these youths as 'Edelweiss Pirates'. Gangs were made up of boys and girls who listened to banned music, smoked and danced. They ridiculed the Hitler Youth by changing the words of their songs and occasionally clashed with them in the streets.

Education

'The whole function of education is to create Nazis.'

Bernhard Rust, Reich Minister of Education.

In Nazi Germany, education meant indoctrination. Hitler used the schools to reinforce Nazi ideas and to teach young people about such things as racial hygiene, the glories of Germany's past and the benefits of physical fitness. Lessons began and ended with the teacher and the students saluting and saying 'Heil Hitler.' The school curriculum was dominated by subjects which served the Nazi purpose. German, Physical Education, History and Biology were given special emphasis. Nazi themes were presented through every subject. Science focused on chemical warfare and explosives, Maths problems dealt with

4

A question taken from a Maths textbook:

Question 95: The construction of a lunatic asylum costs 6 million Marks. (a) How many houses at 15,000 Marks each could have been built for that amount? According to conservative estimates, there are 300,000 mentally ill, epileptics etc., in care. (b) How much do these people cost to keep in total, at a cost of 4 Marks per head? (c) How many marriage loans at 100 Marks each...could be granted from this money?

social issues and artillery calculations and Geography lessons were used to show how Germany was surrounded by hostile neighbours. Textbooks were re-written to reflect and promote Nazi ideas.

The teaching profession was one of the first to be purged of Jews, Socialists and other 'undesirables'. By 1937, a mixture of propaganda and intimidation had succeeded in bringing 97 per cent of German teachers into the Nazi Teachers League. Teachers were required to promote Nazi ideas and values in the classroom and thousands were sent on training courses to prepare

them for their new political role. There was surprisingly little resistance from the teachers. Most were nationalists and conservatives by choice and many had disapproved of the Weimar Republic. It was only later that teachers began to criticise the Nazis when they failed to keep their promises to improve the training and status of teachers.

The Nazis established a network of schools outside the State system. These were designed as training schools for Germany's future leaders. The National Political Educational Institutes (Napolas) were for students aged between 10 and 18. They were run by the SS (after 1936) and trained leaders for the military and the administration. Adolf Hitler Schools were set up to provide future Party leaders. The best students from these schools went to the 'Order Castles' where they endured an exhausting regime of political indoctrination and physical training. These schools were supposed to produce the elite leaders of the future Nazi State.

5

Typical weekly study timetable for a Berlin schoolgirl aged 13

Period	Monday	Tuesday	Wednesday	Thursday	Friday	Saturday
8.00-8.45	German	German	German	German	German	German
8.50-9.35	Geography	History	Singing	Geography	History	Singing
9.40-10.25	Race Study	Race Study	Race Study	Race Study	Party Beliefs	Party Beliefs
10.25-11.00	Break	Break	Break	Break	Break	Break
11.00-12.05	Domestic Science with Maths	Domestic Science with Maths	Domestic Science with Maths	Domestic Science with Maths	Domestic Science with Maths	Domestic Science with Maths
12.10-12.55	Eugenics	Health Biology	Eugenics	Health Biology	Eugenics	Health Biology

During break there would be sports and special announcements.
There was organised sport every afternoon from 2.00 pm - 6.00 pm.

QUESTIONS

1 Why were young people so important to Hitler's plans for Germany?

2 Why did Hitler consider it vital to take control of the German youth movement and the schools?

3 What was the purpose of the activities offered to boys and girls through the Hitler Youth movement?

4 Why did the Nazis encourage children as young as six to join the Hitler Youth?

5 Look at source 1 on page 58. What kind of impression was this type of ritual intended to have on the mind of a ten-year-old boy?

6 Look at source 5. What evidence is there of Nazi indoctrination in this timetable?

7 How successful was the Hitler Youth movement?

The Hitler Youth

SOURCE B

'The discipline of the Hitler Youth in the district of western Germany is very much shaken. Many no longer want to be commanded, but wish to do as they like. Usually only a third of the whole group appears for roll-call.... At evening meetings it is a great event if 20 turn up out of 80, but usually there are only about 10 or 12. The level of these meetings is very low. They sing soldiers' songs and make a lot of noise, without doing any constructive work.'

'Germany Today' magazine, published in Britain in May 1938.

SOURCE A

SOURCE C

'I think one of the worst effects of the whole Nazi youth movement is that our children no longer get any peace and quiet, and I dread to think of the people they will grow up into if they are subject to this incessant thundering of propaganda all the time...we never discuss politics, or the Nazis or their teaching unless the children ask.'

A German mother. This woman was a member of the Confessional Church, one of the few organised opposition groups in Nazi Germany.

SOURCE D

'What I liked about the Hitler Youth was the comradeship. I was full of enthusiasm when I joined the Jungvolk at the age of ten. What boy isn't fired by being presented with high ideals such as comradeship, loyalty and honour. I can still remember how deeply moved I was when we learned the club mottoes: "Jungvolk boys are hard, they can keep a secret, they are loyal; Jungvolk boys are comrades; the highest value for a Jungvolk boy is honour". They seemed to me to be Holy. And then the trips! Is there anything nicer than enjoying the splendours of the homeland in the company of one's comrades.'

The memories of a Hitler Youth leader recorded after World War II.

SOURCE E

'If other people rave about their time as cubs (Pimpfen)...I cannot share their enthusiasm. I have oppressive memories. In our troop the Jungvolk activities consisted almost entirely of stolid military drill. Even if sport or shooting practice or a sing song was scheduled, we always had to do drill first: endless marching with "attention", "at ease", "about turn" ...twelve-year-old leaders bawling out ten-year-old cubs and marching them all over the school play ground...the slightest faults with our uniforms, the slightest lateness on parade were punished with extra drill...Youth must be led by youth was the motto. In practice that meant that those on top could put the boot in.'

Memories of a Hitler Youth member.

QUESTIONS

1 Look at source A. What can a historian learn about the Hitler Youth movement from this photograph?

2 Study source C. How useful would this source be to an historian who wanted to study the reactions of the German people to the Hitler Youth?

3 Look at sources D and E. These sources appear to give very different impressions of life in the Hitler Youth. How would you account for these different interpretations?

4 Study sources A and B. Which of these sources provides the more reliable view of the popularity of the Hitler Youth movement? Explain your answer.

5 Look at all the sources. Using these sources, and your own knowledge how far would it be true to say that all people in Nazi Germany were enthusiastic about the Hitler Youth movement? Explain your answer.

Index